DealMaker Manifesto

The Real Estate Entrepreneur's Guide
To Make Deals and Get Paid

DealMaker Manifesto

The Real Estate Entrepreneur's Guide
To Make Deals and Get Paid

Matt Skinner

Ainsley & Allen
PUBLISHING

Ainsley & Allen Publishing LLC
2035 Sunset Lake Road
Newark, DE 19702
www.ainsleyallenpublishing.com

ISBN-10: 1-946694-11-8
ISBN-13: 978-1-946694-11-9

Library of Congress Control Number: 2017947960

Dedication

To the seekers who were not born with a silver spoon in their mouth; who are willing to put in the work and BECOME something new in order to BE, DO, and HAVE everything you want in life.

This book is for you.

A DealMaker is...

A trailblazer.

A problem solver.

An oath maker.

A warrior in a concrete jungle.

The very essence of the evolutionary spirit.

Are you a DealMaker?

You can be by the time you finish this book.

Acknowledgments

Thank you to my father, Norman "Jay" Skinner who showed me what it is to be a man. If it weren't for his wisdom and guidance, I would not be able to give you this book.

My father is the ultimate man's man. This left-handed carpenter can build a house with his bare hands, restore cars (like the 1970 Mustang Mach 1 I blew the 351 Cleveland out of when I was 16) and never miss a bolt going to the cadmium plater.

He rides classic British motorcycles, flies airplanes, glides on 2x6 water skis and can build a fire with a rock and leaf. And he loves his woman (my mother) with everything he's got.

He gave me a lot to look up to as a boy, and I am tremendously grateful to have such a role model in my life.

When I was a kid, my father left for work wearing nail bags and work boots in his work truck with a big black Great Dane he named Clinton; as soon as I got big enough he took me along, too.

I watched him sell jobs as a general contractor, frame custom houses, and apartment buildings, then transition into going to work in a suit to build whole communities with one of the largest real estate developers in California.

My father is a great conversationalist because he is genuinely curious to learn from anyone in any station of life and he's dangerously smart enough to carry on a conversation on any subject.

He is gifted with a rare form of charisma I think only exists in great world leaders. He's always happy and will reframe any negative circumstance into a positive.

My father is a great man. I know what an advantage I've had in life because of the character he modeled for me.

Everyone who knows him knows he is a rock; he taught me always to do what you say you will do, especially when it's difficult and even when it's no longer in your best interest.

Integrity like his is uncommon, and I am proud to say this is my father's legacy.

FOREWORD
BY RYAN STEWMAN

They say, "A strong man is not afraid to show vulnerability," and in this book, Matt lays it all out on the line in the name of helping people. I've met a lot of people in my lifetime, and I can whole-heartedly tell you Matt is a one-of-a-kind caring man. He cares so much about helping people that in this book he tells some really hard stories about the lessons he's learned, in order to save readers, the pain he's endured.

This is a book of lessons, experience, and perseverance. The book ropes you in right from the first paragraph. Matt wastes no time getting to the good stuff and keeping your attention. Most business books are boring and redundant. By the time you've reached page 100, you still haven't gotten to any kind of point. This book is the opposite of that. After page three, you've already learned the first lesson, and the book keeps stacking the awesomeness from there.

I've personally raised myself from poverty to prosperity using real estate. If everything I knew went out the window tomorrow, I'd go make money with real estate. It's the safest, best investment ever. You make money in bad times. You make money in good times. No matter the market, you can't lose if you know how to play the game.

This book is the handbook to the game of real estate investing. I've watched Matt buy up property after property. His portfolio spans multiple states, and his returns are some of the best I've ever seen. Matt is experienced, educated and able to navigate through tough real estate deals with ease. The man with the plan—Matt Skinner.

Real estate is all about making deals. Deals include more than just price. When you buy real estate, you are looking for two parts to qualify it as a deal. Part one is the price. Part two is the terms of the deal. You can overpay for a property, but if the deal is done right, you will still make money from it. That's the beauty of real estate; if you learn the lessons in this book, you can't lose.

After you read this book, you're going to be faced with a decision. You're going to have to decide to invest in real estate and more importantly, invest in real estate with Matt Skinner. There are a lot of real estate gurus out there. Most of them don't even own the house they live in. Hell, from what I can tell, Matt is the only real estate trainer who still has hair. Just sayin'. No one should take advice from hairless trainers.

The point of this book is to educate you on real estate investing and to compel you to take action and start building your portfolio. The best time to invest in real estate is right now. Which brings me to my last point: it's important to read the book, but education is useless without implementation. If you read this book and it inspires you to start investing, hit Matt up, he's the best, and he'll help you implement what you've learned.

Lastly, I'd like to say it's a great honor to know Matt Skinner. He's a sharp guy with a solid understanding of this thing we call life. I'm honored to have him as a friend, a client and someone I look up to. You're gonna love this book, and you're gonna love Matt.

Table of Contents

Introduction

I was sitting in traffic when the fateful text message came through.

"I can't fund the deal we discussed because I have to fly overseas and won't have the time to make that happen."

My heart sank.

Three days before, I had put up $50,000 of my own money as a non-refundable deposit on an apartment building. I had nine days to close, and my "partner" was backing out at the last minute.

A few months earlier, I had made an offer on a 32-unit apartment building that had been foreclosed on and was now owned by FDIC. A major brokerage had listed it for $1.25 million, and I offered $930,000. I remember how the broker erupted in a flurry of cursing accusing me of being "new" (which was true) for writing such a "low-ball" offer. Then after falling out of escrow a few times with other buyers, he called back to see if I was still interested.

Of course, I was.

It was 2009, and the real estate market had just collapsed. House prices were still free-falling, and many people had very little faith in real estate in general. But I knew that the best time to buy is when things are on sale...and this deal was definitely on sale. At my offer price, this was a clearance sale. Buying an asset that can be made to cash flow at the bottom of the market and then riding the wave of appreciation to the top to sell is the most fundamental way to make money.

At $930,000 this 32-unit was a steal!

It took everything inside me to say, "Because you took so long to get back to me, my partners and I have moved on and are doing other projects."

The broker let out a few more expletives and asked, "What do you need?"

I mustered everything I had and replied coldly "The best I can do is $850,000 to be interested."

Silence.

Then another storm of cuss words flew out of the broker's mouth.

When the tantrum finally ended, he said he needed to call the bank to find out what their position was. I got a call back minutes later with a counter offer of $865,000 —a 30% discount off their original ask price—and I faked reluctance as I agreed to move forward with the deal.

At this point, my heart was pounding in my chest. I knew this was a home run at $930,000 and even a grand slam at $865,000.

I went home that day and gathered all the available cash I could put together to come up with the non-refundable deposit of $50,000 to lock up the deal.

I had already made a deal with a guy who promised to partner with me by putting up the rest of the cash.

Three days later, I got the fateful text message from that so-called "partner" who backed out.

Damn.

If I didn't come up with the rest of the money, I would lose my $50,000 and the deal.

I had no choice but to make it happen.

MAKE DEALS AND GET PAID

A lot of people take real estate classes, and they learn techniques and strategies of how to do real estate. Heck, real estate training is a multi-billion-dollar industry in and of itself. You can get a college degree, even an MBA in real estate.

But compared to the amount of people who study real estate—go to college, take weekend seminars, read books, blogs, even dabble in real estate on weekends—

why are there so few true DealMakers in the world? Real DealMakers.

Most people who study real estate can make a great living in the industry: as a real estate agent, broker, loan officer, escrow, title, educator...

But it takes more than just a general knowledge of how-to-do real estate to make it as a real estate entrepreneur. In fact, it takes a special set of skills to become a DealMaker.

A DealMaker is a real estate entrepreneur who can make deals when no one else believes one is possible; one who can see the highest and best use for a property where no one else would dare to look, and most of all, one who can pull it together when the deal is seemingly falling apart all around him.

A DealMaker makes things happen; especially when its difficult.

People with money (investors) only want to invest with DealMakers (elite real estate entrepreneurs) who know how to solve problems, who know what to do when the shit hits the fan and will have the sand to take care of business when the going gets tough.

Smart investors know the best use of their time is doing what they are best at (their career or profession) and choose to invest only with true professional DealMakers.

Institutions, pension funds, insurance companies, and other very smart money managers invest with DealMakers; they don't try to learn how to DO real estate themselves. They hire the best negotiators, promoters, marketers, and managers to invest with.

In this book, I am going to take you through all the skill sets it takes to BE a DealMaker.

I call these specific skill-sets The Five Pillars of Deal Making.

The Five Pillars are not something you can master just from reading one book, but this book will give you a road map to WHO you need to BECOME in order to Make Deals and Get Paid. And that's the kind of person (entrepreneur) you will need to BE in order to attract investors and capital into your business.

The Five Pillars will require a lifetime commitment to master but let me tell you it will be worth it.

I have been on this path for most of my life. Yet I continue to learn something new every day. But that's what makes being a DealMaker the best pursuit on the planet.

Because I have practiced these five principles, I was able to weather the worst crash in financial history and come out the other side with a thriving investment firm.

It's all about who you have to BE or become in order DO and HAVE all the things you want in life.

The good news is none of the skills that make up the Five Pillars are talents that only some people can attain. Anyone with the will and the drive can master the Five Pillars and become a DealMaker.

To become a DealMaker, you must master the Five Pillars of Deal Making:

1. Marketing

2. Salesmanship

3. Negotiation

4. Business Systems

5. Financial Intelligence

This book will give you many real-world real estate scenarios that I have been involved with; from feeling like I had the Midas touch to weathering through downturns in the market, I will share with you the value of what becoming a DealMaker has enabled me to accomplish. My mission is to give you the tools to be a DealMaker, too—so you can go anywhere, and under any circumstance Make Deals and Get Paid.

This book's primary focus will be on the most important factor that can make you a big success. We will focus on YOU.

We will focus on who you need to BE in order DO and HAVE everything you want in life.

I write this book from my high-rise condo overlooking the Pacific Ocean in Marina del Rey, California. I have a killer sports car in the garage 10 floors below and a beautiful woman who challenges me and inspires me to be my best every day. I have three beautiful children who are healthy, happy, and so smart. I have a prosperous real estate business and a great team of DealMakers that I have trained.

Honestly, I have everything I want in life...

But I certainly didn't start out this way.

I am going to share with you the trials and tribulations that made me the DealMaker I am today; but first, how I saved my little 32-unit apartment deal...

SAVING THE DEAL

After receiving that fateful call, I pulled over to the side of the road. I opened my phone and began scrolling through all the contacts I had in there marked INV for investor. Most of these people at the time had not invested with me before, so calling on each of them was not only time consuming but a complete crap shoot.

But I had a great deal. And you make money when you buy, not when you sell, so I was confident that this deal would make sense to somebody on that list.

I sat in my truck under the 101 Freeway in Los Angeles that day for what was probably an hour or more, listening to both the traffic whiz by my driver's side door and rumble above me on the freeway overpass.

I must have dialed a hundred numbers *feeling more and more anxious as each moment passed. There was no room for failure. The economy was terrible, and I definitely could not afford to lose a dollar—let alone $50,000. My life and my children depended on me.*

Thank God, I had built my network before I needed all those prospective investors I'd saved in my phone.

I spoke to a quite a few potential investors that day and then booked meetings with two of them for the next day at a local coffee shop.

Satisfied but not settled, I drove home.

The next day, I brought my "A" game. I had a property information package and investment prospectus. I was prepared to make the pitch and had all the details of the deal spelled out clearly and simply for my investor to see because that's what investors want.

I needed over a million dollars in about a week.

My worst fear was that someone I contacted would smell the blood in the water and steal my deal.

That day I met with both prospective investors and gave them my pitch. Then I showed them all the information and due diligence I had on the deal and explained what was in it for them if they made the investment with me.

And guess what? Both said Yes!

Both wanted to see the property, so I lined it up for the following day.

Tick tock, tick tock...now down to seven days to fund and close, or I would lose my $50,000 non-refundable deposit.

My faith in my DealMaking ability gave me the confidence that this was a special deal and so I gave the property tours with gusto.

Again, both prospective investors said yes.

And now, I had a new dilemma: which investor to trust as a new partner.

I made my decision, and I made the right one.

One investor wanted a little more than I had originally offered but I trusted him more to do what he said he would do and so instead of allowing my greed gland to take over, I went with the more trustworthy partner and made the deal with him.

We shook hands and made promises to one another. Then I sent a summary to my attorney to draft up the agreement.

My new partner did what he said he would do, and I did what I said I would do.

The deal ended up being a success. Just the way I planned it.

We purchased the property for $865,000, and we put about $200,000 in repairs into it.

The empty but newly remodeled 32-unit property leased up in about 45 days (way ahead of my projections), and it began to cash flow.

Once the property had stabilized with renters, it appraised for almost $1.7 million.

At that point, we refinanced which allowed the investor to get 100 percent of his money out plus some proceeds from the loan; and the asset cash flows to this day.

This is what we consider a grand slam.

When you can get 100 percent of your invested principal out of a deal (and then some) and continue to own the asset for all of its benefits: cash flow, tax benefits, appreciation, mortgage interest deductions, and growth; you can't get better than an infinite return.

Since this deal, I have hit several grand slams *and quite a few triples* which we'll discuss later in this book. And I will show you how to do it too.

I love apartment investing in this way because of all the reasons listed above, but I especially like these kinds of deals because of what it takes to make it happen.

From Ditches to Riches

I was fortunate. As a young man, I knew what I wanted to become. I knew what I wanted in life. I knew I wanted to become a real estate developer like Donald Trump. I had a background in construction, and I hail from a long line of contractors. My dad is a contractor. His brothers are contractors. Both my grandfathers were contractors. It runs deep in my blood.

Many years before I acquired the "grand slam" property (or any property at all) I was a broke kid digging ditches for a plumbing contractor to pay my rent.

My career started right out of high school in the trenches. Literally.

The plumbing contractor I was working for was smart, very well off, and commanded a lot of respect. I was young, muscular and tan, so I was content digging ditches for him, which shows you the extent of my goals at the time. But I knew I wanted to be like him one day. I wanted to be the boss.

The owner came out to the job site one day. Like every other day, I was just digging away, working hard. He walked over to me and said,

"Hey Mr. Skinner, how's that shovel fit in your hand?"

His abrupt question stopped me in my tracks, and like a bolt of lightning through my heart, I had an epiphany.

It was at that moment I realized my shovel was the only tool I had to provide for myself. It was my only means to feed myself, make my car payment, pay my rent, buy catsup and mustard and all that real-life stuff. I didn't want to be *"that"* guy; the guy with only **one tool** to make a living.

When I heard that question, I instantly knew I needed to get a **better toolbox**. I needed multiple streams of income and multiple opportunities to go into the world and fix things. When you know how to fix things, your value has no limits. That one little comment, intended or not, lit a fire under my ass. I realized I had a lot to learn, and it would take several years to go from digging ditches to making multimillion-dollar deals in the real estate world, but I was dedicated and ready to start my journey.

I spent the next two years designing my life. I read books on goal setting, manifesting, and going after what I wanted. I also devoured books on real estate and construction and designed a plan to achieve my goals.

I wanted to be the boss, the guy who shows up in a suit and tie and tells people what to do. I mapped out what that would look like, and then I reverse engineered it. I made an actionable plan on how I would go about accomplishing it, but I still had to start at the bottom, or so I thought at the time.

Over the next couple of years, I got my contractor's license and landed a better job in construction than digging ditches, but I still wasn't the "BOSS" that I knew my destiny demanded of me.

The Best Way to Make Money is to Work for Free

At the ripe age of 22, I got fired from my position as Project Manager for a custom home builder in Los Angeles. *At first, I was devastated. I was angry. "How dare they fire ME of all people?"*

I thought I knew everything then—and looking back it's difficult to believe such a well-established company even hired such a kid to manage their projects.

I thought to myself I could either commit to finding another job, or I could go out and find a project, start my own business.

And that's exactly what I did.

With the dream of one day becoming a real estate developer, I set out on the first step of my journey and started a construction company.

Just me and a truck full of tools, I was off to make my mark.

I went to my grandfather's house because he'd agreed to let me use his fax machine, and I faxed out a flyer I'd made on the computer saying I was a contractor and open for business.

To my surprise, I landed my first project soon after that and began my career as a builder.

I began remodeling a decent size home in the Encino Hills, a little suburb just north of Los Angeles in the Valley. I worked hard, striving every day to meet my client's needs and wants.

At first, it started with a few small projects on my client's home and then turned into a major remodel. I almost completely tore down the entire house only to rebuild it.

My first client gave me a referral, and before I knew it, I had three projects going in the same neighborhood.

I knew then that I couldn't possibly run all those projects myself while simultaneously selling new work.

At that point in my career, I was fortunate to have the wisdom to realize I wasn't an expert yet at managing the projects and the day-to-day stuff that goes with it: "Is the plumber going to show up? Did the electrician call in sick?", etc.

What I did realize is that I was a pretty darn good salesmen and I had a knack for showing up on time (doing what you say you will do will get you a long way in life, and especially in a city like LA) I provided excellent customer service, and always did what I promised.

I think that my salesmanship skills came from some of my childhood experiences. In elementary school, I would go door-to-door soliciting the people that lived in my neighborhood to wash their cars or walk their dogs for money. I had to sell them on giving me the job.

Later, I wanted to buy a remote-controlled car that cost hundreds of dollars. My parents were not going to buy that extravagant of a gift for me so I knew if I wanted to have that car I would have to work for it. I applied for a job with the local newspaper and got myself a paper route. Each morning, I would get up a 5:00 a.m. and fold and rubber band the papers that were dropped at my door then I would walk my hilly neighborhood throwing papers on driveways and doorsteps. (I tried riding my bike like the kids in the movies but ended up pushing my bike up the hills because they were too steep to pedal up). At that time, the newspaper's policy was that everyone got the paper and that payment was voluntary. So, once a month, I would go around door-to-door and knock and ask for the $4.25 that was the suggested monthly (voluntary) subscription. I had to sell my clients who were receiving the free paper on why they should pay me for delivery. And sell I did.

Three months into owning my own construction business, I made the most important (and risky) business decision of my career.

I knew if I managed my current projects that, after all the income and expenses and start-up costs, I would be able to pay myself a wage commensurate with a $50,000 salary.

I also knew that if I didn't get out and market and sell new work that in a few months I would be jobless again.

So, I decided to double down and take 100 percent of what I was paying myself, forego any pay for 90 days, and hire someone more experienced than me to run my current projects: a manager.

That was a big risk for me at the time. I was young, single, and had no other sources of income. It was the early 2000's, and we had just experienced the market crash as the dot-com bubble burst.

I had to work for free for a few months in order to hire someone better than me, but this would free up my time to go bid projects and sell more work to grow the company.

I would play to my strong suit.

I hired a guy named Scott—an old salty dog who had a billion years' experience running projects. He had been a contractor (like me) once upon a time, but like most contractors had gotten burned out running the business side of marketing and selling to get the next project.

Together we made a perfect team because all he wanted to do was run jobs, and all I wanted to do was market and sell and run a business.

I was happy to let Scott handle the day-to-day details of project management while I went out and grew my network, meeting people, and selling them on hiring a young kid to remodel and later build their dream houses.

I gave myself 90 days with Scott; worst case scenario I would eat Top Ramen while I paid all my profits to Scott to run the projects. This was me burning my ships. Failure was not an option.

If I didn't go out and find more work, Scott and I would both suffer.

So, that's exactly what I did.

In my first year in business, I did over a million dollars in business. And in the next several years, I built a general contracting business doing nearly $10 million in revenue consistently each year. Soon, I found I had three Scott's running my jobs, a cool office in Encino, and over 50 employees.

I was the BOSS.

But I still had the dream of being in real estate—in fact, to be a real estate developer—to be the BOSS of that kind of enterprise.

And that's when I doubled down again.

$5,000 INTO MILLIONS

Not long after I hired Scott, I saw a billboard for a seminar featuring all these real estate gurus who were going to speak in LA.

I had to go.

I took the day off work to learn about real estate investing and watched as they paraded the guys out one after another to pitch their real estate investing programs.

I remember when I saw my first mentor on stage.

He was disheveled.

He was old.

He was crass.

He was a salty dog.

My kind of person.

I loved his off-color humor and politically incorrect way of communicating. He said he had been a carny (that's carnival worker for those of you in Rio Linda) in a "past life" before becoming a successful real estate investor, and he promised to show me how to make money in real estate with no money or credit.

I was sold!

I ran to the back of the room and maxed out two credit cards to be able to attend his $5,000 event; and yeah, it took two credit cards for me at that time. I mean five grand might as well have been a million because I simply didn't have it.

But I made the investment in myself.

I wanted more than anything to know what he knew and to be able to do what he did.

I wanted to Make Deals and Get Paid.

I wanted to flip houses and amass a real estate portfolio just like he had talked about. Ultimately, I wanted to be a real estate developer!

I was so excited about my investment in myself that I called my girlfriend at the time and told her about the investment I had just made in my myself. She laughed at me and told me I'd just gotten scammed.

Fortunately, I was still sold on the seminar because I ignored her and beamed from ear to ear about the new path I was about to take.

Several weeks later, I attended a four-day workshop and learned about wholesaling, creative financing, fix and flips and short sales. At this point, I had zero real estate experience. It was like a dream. It felt like drinking out of firehose there was so much information to take in.

I learned the tips and techniques on how to transact real estate at this event, but most importantly I learned how to market.

This guy was a master marketer and I not only implemented his strategies to make real estate deals, but I also implemented them in my construction business. I still use some of his tactics to this day and I teach them to my Dealmaker's in my DealMaker Society.

Maybe because I was naive enough to believe every word he said I took everything I learned there and just did it. I didn't ask questions or try to make his system better. I just did it.

In several short weeks, I'd took that first $5,000 investment in myself and turned it into $13,000! I did my first real estate deal and I was hooked!

Not only was that a fantastic ROI (return on investment) for that class, but it gave me the faith and courage to know this stuff really worked, and I was hooked 100 percent on doing real estate as my life path.

Unknowingly, I had begun the journey of mastering the Five Pillars.

I had a great foundation as a salesman; I was honing my marketing and negotiation skills, and I had begun working as a manager of people and systems.

But I still had a lot to learn.

THRIVE

As I continued learning from books, audio recordings, and mentors, my construction company took off—we were building huge custom homes in places like Bel Air, Malibu, and Hollywood Hills—for people whose names you would recognize.

At the same time, I continued marketing to find real estate deals, buying fixer houses, and flipping them and acquiring rental houses. I did a lot of deals.

When I realized bigger projects were less risky than smaller projects, I began organizing investors for development projects.

THINK BIG

Buying junker houses, fixing them up and selling them is risky business. It's risky even for a guy who has spent years as a real estate developer, a house flipper, and a general contractor. Even now, I find fixer houses to be high-risk projects. What I've found is that when I do development projects, I'm able to mitigate a lot of my risk because everything is designed on paper first and I know everything that has to do with the land.

As a developer, I determine what the highest and best use for the land is. I build it in my mind first, then translate it onto paper with the help of an architect and engineers. And then we go through a process: we check, we double check, we engineer, we re-engineer; the city checks it, and everything goes forward. We have civil engineers, structural engineers, architects, geologist, surveyors, all these pieces that go into designing a new building product—a new building—and everything is double checked and triple checked, which makes development a less risky proposition.

It just takes more capital to get started in development. It takes experience. I'll tell you, if you have an experienced developer and you have the capital to pull off a project, development is a relatively low-risk investment that can deliver tremendous returns based on the experience, the know-how, and a get-shit-done attitude. When people invest with me in my development projects, that's exactly what they get.

Today, my firm does two kinds of deals. We do development, and we buy apartment buildings.

I used to buy fix-and-flip houses; make a profit, and reinvest in rental houses.

Now, I've graduated to developing property in some of the most prestigious areas of the world and owning and operating a portfolio of apartment assets.

I buy apartment buildings in emerging US markets. It's been a fantastic strategy for us. When you graduate from flipping little junker houses and buying little rental houses that make you a landlord, you're moving up and will only keep going up. You get into a bigger game, with bigger profits and less risk, an investor's dream.

Boyle Heights

Years ago, I bought a house from a wholesaler who I had trained.

Wholesaling is the technique of creating a great deal, tying it up, and flipping the contract to someone who has the money to make the deal happen. Buying from a wholesaler is a good way to get additional deal flow and I still buy deals from wholesalers. Wholesaling is also a great way to get started in the real estate investment business before you have your own money make any significant purchases.

This deal I purchased from the wholesaler was a short sale on a duplex in a rough part of Los Angeles called Boyle Heights. The house was old, maybe built in the 1930's, which is really old for LA.

I did all the normal inspections on the house including hiring a third-party inspector to check for termites, etc.

I always use a third party to inspect my properties before I buy them even though I am a fully licensed general contractor and technically able to save that money. I take the approach that a third party will be impartial in their inspection and give me unbiased eyes on the deal. I like that because it mitigates risk.

On this particular deal, we got all our third-party inspections done and closed on the property.

My intent was to fix it up cosmetically, sell it for retail price, and make a handsome profit.

The first day on the job, we tore out some of the lath and plaster and quickly discovered that termites had whittled their way through nearly 90 percent of the framing—so much so that the lath and plaster and exterior stucco were the only things holding up the house!

It was going to be a huge expense to replace all of that structure, and the city would normally require us to tear down the entire house and have it all reengineered from the ground up to rebuild.

Most entrepreneurs would probably have gone weak in the knees and bailed.

But I spent the next several weeks negotiating with the city to let me replace the termite infested framing and forego the re-engineering and costly rebuild. They agreed, and I strapped on my nail bags and did most of the framing myself to save money.

The project did run over budget and took longer than expected, but we got the job done and sold the house for a profit.

This would not have been possible if I had not purchased the property with such a profit margin cushion that it could withstand unforeseen problems.

Another takeaway was that my investor on this deal discovered the real reason that people invest with me: as a trained professional, I make things happen, even when the odds are stacked against me. I used my skills and ability to negotiate a compromise with the city and to get things done. I make sure I do this even when life throws a curve ball.

It's risky business to invest with someone with limited experience.

In the real estate investing business, unforeseen things happen to the best of us; what sets me apart is my ability to deploy the skills I have gained from the Five Pillars and my uncanny ability to get things done in the face of adversity.

The Five Pillars

To be a success in business you need to learn how to be a great marketer; you need to learn how to sell; you need to learn how to negotiate; you need to be able to manage your time, your life, and the people who work for you, as well as you need to know how to manage systems that make things easy for you. Ultimately, you must have financial intelligence.

These are the Five Pillars that we're going to go through in this book.

1. Marketing

2. Sales

3. Negotiation

4. Management

5. Financial Intelligence

I've also included some real estate tips, tricks, and techniques. Most importantly, I want you to know that you can take all the real estate courses on techniques and strategies that you want, but if you don't work on the Five Pillars for yourself, it will be near impossible to achieve success in any entrepreneurial role.

I hope what you take from this book is the foundation of who you need to BE in order to DO and HAVE all the things you want in your life.

You are the writer of your own script.

You are the director of your own play.

Then, and only then, will you become the actor on the stage of life.

Most people think they are JUST the actor, cast in a role they cannot change or have no power over; they just play the hand they're given and recite the lines they think are written for them.

But that's all bullshit.

Today is a new day. The only thing that matters is now.

You write the script of your future.

You determine the role you get to play on the stage called life.

And then you get to act it out every single day in a beautiful presentation.

I'm going to tell you...it's not easy. It's a lot of responsibility not to play the victim.

The first time I really dove into this mindset, and fully took responsibility for my life, I had to change so many things, from my friends, to my mindset, to who I was looking up to and following. I had to change my mentors and even my zip code along the way. Moving to a new town was part of achieving the success I wanted. You may need to do these things to reach your success. It's up to you. It's all a choice.

That's the amazing thing about this country. You have the freedom to write your own script, direct your own life, and act out the role you choose for yourself each and every day. Nothing can hold you back.

Play the part every day that you have designed for yourself. That's the essence of Freedom. This is what the American dream really is.

You have the power to BE, DO and HAVE everything you want in this life.

Pillar I: Marketing

Great Deals Are Made—Not Found

If you're serious about being a DealMaker, you can't wait and hope that some realtor is going to put your best interest ahead of theirs and bring you the best deals. Because they never will.

You've got to be a marketer and attract motivated sellers to you, so that you can listen directly to what their pain points are and solve their problem directly. Making great deals is the art of solving your seller's problem.

Marketing is making friends and giving them value.

***

MY FIRST MARKETING CAMPAIGN

Five grand in debt with a headful of amazing information, I set out on my journey to make a deal and get paid.

I selected a geo-target (area of focus) and then began a mailing campaign to attract motivated sellers by mailing them a simple post card.

It didn't take long, and my phone was ringing...

"Hello? I got your postcard in the mail that says you buy houses?"

Holly shit! It worked!

Now, what???

I did my very first real estate deal from one of the leads from my very first campaign.

Edna had called me; she was a sweet old lady who had bought a house for her sons to live in. They trashed the place and never paid her rent.

She was behind a couple of payments but had some equity in the house.

I drove out to meet Edna and offered to take over ownership of the property "Subject To" meaning, I would take the deed and title the property "as-is" and promise to make the payments on her loan (which would remain in her name.)

So, I met Edna at the house and had a traveling notary come with me. I explained how my offer would work and Edna signed the deed over to me on the spot with No Money Down!

Holly shit, again! It's working!

Edna then asked me to follow her to Home Depot so she could make a copy of the keys. (I don't know why she wanted to keep a key to a house she didn't own anymore, but I was so jazzed about the whole thing I didn't even think about it).

I just remember following her in my beat up pick-up truck, tools rattling in the back all the way to Home Depot, which was only a few miles away. I was TERRIFIED that ol' Edna was going to speed off with the only key to my house! Ha. Catch that? _My House..._

I flipped that house to another investor a few weeks later for **$13,000**. To me, at that time, it may as well have been a billion dollars.

I was hooked. I knew that I could go out there and do that same process again.

And again.

And again.

More than anything else, I realized this stuff is easy.

The real estate part is so easy.

If you know how to market yourself; know how to sell an idea, negotiate a win-win outcome and have a reasonable understanding of financial intelligence, you can do anything. Including...

Make Deals and Get Paid.

I expanded my toolbox that day. I used to have only a shovel, but now my toolbox was expanding.

I still employ the same strategies I learned from that first real estate course, and I've built upon them.

I've bought multimillion dollar apartment buildings with the same "Subject To" strategy I just described and have wholesaled land and commercial real estate for fees higher than six figures.

I learned and put into practice the basic marketing principles I am now showing you in this book.

I'll start by introducing you to you my all-powerful "Rule of 92," and I'll teach you how to create a "Target Marketing System," that attracts more motivated sellers than you may know what to do with...yet.

THE DEALMAKER MARKETING PHILOSOPHY

DealMakers believe that marketing is simply making friends and **consistently** giving them value. It's discovering a friendship and cultivating that relationship with the intent of transacting in the future. We must build a group of friends that are willing and able to buy what you have for sale or have something that you want to buy. Dealmaker Marketing is not only focusing on making the sale but improving lives.

THE RULE OF 92

One of the biggest mistakes real estate investors (and nearly all realtors) make is diluting their marketing efforts. Many would-be buyers or listing agents looking for motivated sellers will market in one part of town for a while and then move to another entirely different market as soon as Aunt Sally gives them a referral over there. This is the equivalent of pissing in the ocean; instantly diluted and forgotten.

All real estate entrepreneurs need to know that statistically, 92 percent of all properties sell within seven years. If you concentrate on a list of 500 properties, 460 will sell over a 7-year time span. Continuing with those metrics, nearly 6 of the 500 will transact any given month. If you identify a specific target market with 500 target properties (you want to buy), then you should statistically have the opportunity to buy 5 or 6 deals each month, if you're consistent with your marketing.

That's a lot of transactions, especially when you're doing multimillion dollar deals. Just imagine if you could get 1 out of 6; if you are marketing well, you should be getting 4 or 5 qualified sellers a month from your list of 500 targets...again, if you are consistent with it.

Take a step back and think about if you are constantly marketing, calling, emailing, using direct mail and postcards, sending fancy little Hallmark-type envelopes that come to their house, and targeting them on social media. They're in your group; they're in your club; they know who you are. You've got rapport; you've built a relationship, and when they want to sell, why wouldn't they call you when they know that you are a closer and that you do what you say you're going to do? Once people know that you're a closer, they will want to do business with you.

Go Deep, Not Wide

Beware of becoming a shallow marketer. DealMakers must create sincere, mutually beneficial relationships with potential sellers which are going to translate into business. What does shallow marketing look like? I'm glad you asked.

Most real estate agents get a referral to sell Aunt Sally's house on one side of town, so they do a little bit of marketing around her house while that one house is listed for sale and maybe in escrow. After that closes, they forget about all those people they just marketed to. They don't develop a relationship. They don't go deep. They don't develop a rapport with that group. Instead, Aunt Sally or some other family member refers them to Uncle John's place that's in another town 30 miles away. Then they go over to that side of town and they start doing their little marketing campaign in that area and send out their mailers. That's shallow.

The problem with this real estate agent selling Aunt Sally's and Uncle John's houses is that they've diluted their marketing strategy by changing the list of people they're targeting. You definitely want to be cautious that you don't do that.

By the way, I know that as you read this, you are probably thinking of the times that you've committed this cardinal sin. It's nothing to be ashamed of. I've been guilty of it too, but I'll tell you, what works is being consistent with your marketing and putting clear attention on your intentions.

DealMaker Targeting System

To get the most from your marketing efforts, get clear on who your Target Market is.

Start by identifying the geographic area that you want to own in, and continue to focus in by deciding the exact type of asset class that you want to go after.

For example, in 2009 I decided my Target Market would be San Antonio, Texas because they were one of the only cities in the country that were creating jobs at that time. I decided I wanted to buy apartment buildings there. Then I chose the side of town that was best suited for my investors and me.

I obtained a list of 500 addresses of apartment buildings that I wanted to own, then skip traced the owners of those properties and made them my friends.

I called them each month.

I mailed them a letter each month.

I emailed them interesting articles I found about apartment ownership, the economy, and tax benefits that I'd found.

These days, I even add my Target Market list to my social media.

What I don't do is just bomb them with solicitations. I give them value first. I let them know what I do. They call me when they know I can help them... Like a friend. Like a favor.

Wouldn't you like to be in the position of being a friend doing a favor for your seller? Would that give you a comfortable position to negotiate from?

By the way, 500 Targets can be mailed for about $250/ month. Calls are free. The lists of owners are free in most states through a title company. And skip trace software is less than $30/month. You really have no excuses.

STEP #1: TARGET GEOGRAPHY

The targeting system begins with a geographic area. Basically, just ask yourself, where is the best place for you to buy? If you're starting out completely new, most people start in their own backyard just to make it easy.

But once you are 100 percent committed to being a professional DealMaker, I recommend choosing your

Target Market based on job growth and a healthy economy. Research what cities are growing, what cities are adding jobs, what cities are attracting business. When businesses grow, housing follows. Look for a combination of low taxes, low regulation, low cost of living, and a reasonable labor cost which usually attracts business to the area and in turn creates more jobs. More jobs mean a growing demand for housing, and there you go with the trickle-down effect. I look for those kinds of trends in the marketplace when I choose my geographic Target Market.

STEP #2: TARGET ASSET CLASS

Next, you want to define which asset class you're targeting. There are all kinds of different asset classes that you can choose from. You can choose flipping junker houses, buying pretty houses with terms, apartments, value-add deals, land, commercial, industrial, and much more. None of them are right or wrong, just different. They all have their benefits and their downsides, except for apartments, in my opinion. Apartments are my personal preference because of their low risk, tax advantages, cash flow, and forced appreciation.

STEP #3: TARGET OWNERS

Once you've selected the geographic area and asset class, DealMakers must generate (or purchase) a list of all the owners of those assets. I encourage you to spend the time and effort in this beginning stage creating and scrutinizing your list closely. Occasionally, you may have to penetrate a company, a corporation, a partnership name, or a trust where title is held to find out who owns it.

Once you know who owns the assets in the market that you want to buy, do your due diligence on them; make a list. This is your Target; who you are Hunting.

Step #4: Target Owner Personalities

We could even narrow that down and add a special circumstance to your Target Market; say we only want to buy properties from people getting divorced; or we choose pre-foreclosure or properties that have loans maturing; we could choose sellers who live out of state, or who have a high net worth or a low net worth.

Whatever your target is, make that clear decision.

Remember, there are also people who just don't want their properties anymore. They might have a financial situation; they may have filed for bankruptcy, or they may have other personal burdens like a health issue financially hurting them. They may need the money from the sale of their property to take care of those concerns. In many cases, they're just ready to trade up.

Motivation to sell does not always require a negative situation to the Seller.

Targeting System Closing

You've decided your Target Market. You've developed your list. You're doing your marketing campaign, adding value to your Target Market's lives. Make sure you develop rapport and a relationship with your Targets that will generate business for you.

Even if you're just a real estate agent looking to list, this is exactly how you should do it. In fact, as DealMakers, we look at real estate agents as our competition. I want to get to a seller before a real estate agent does, this way they don't screw up my deal and get in between me and a seller, who I always want to negotiate with on a direct, one-on-one basis.

Real estate agents are not bad people; I just don't need or want someone with less skill negotiating on my behalf. Ever.

Now that you've identified your Target Market through geography, asset class, owners and even their personalities you must decide WHAT you are going to use to target them. Now we must generate "Content Creation" and tackle the "Marketing Whip."

Engage with Content

Remember, marketing is just making friends and adding value. When you can create value-driven content, you'll engage your audience. In your infancy state as a marketer, you'll be tempted to talk all about yourself and how great you are and why people should do business with you. And then as you mature, your focus will be genuinely on how you can help others. Consequently, you'll attract your tribe; you'll engage your people, and they will feel comfortable doing business with you because they will trust you for being authentic.

Recently, I've been aggressively buying apartment buildings and wanted to grow our Target Market offerings. What did I do to accomplish this? I created a social media group entitled "Apartment Investors Association" that features great information about being an apartment owner and improving your apartment cash flow. The engaging content attracts more qualified owners to our group, and in return, this gives me a larger audience, or group of people who know me, trusts me, and sees my content. They know that it's safe, secure and stable (not to mention fun and easy) to do business with me. When I have something for sale, they're like a pool of hungry fish fighting over getting involved with what we've got. Whether it's a deal we're trying sell, or it's an investment opportunity for them to get involved in; even when I'm buying I'm really selling, aren't I?

There are options on what you can do to build your audience. You can have a mail list, a Facebook group, a LinkedIn group, Instagram followers, whatever works for you. No matter your approach, you need to build a Target Market group of people who know who you are, trust who you are, and to whom you've demonstrated you can provide value way before you've asked them buy, sell, or invest with you.

THE MARKETING WHIP

The Marketing Whip is a pattern you've knowingly or unknowingly seen on TV for decades, which has been developed by brilliant marketers at TV stations.

On TV, they give you value through their programming; meaning, the show you want to watch. They give value on about a four-to-one ratio which means they'll show the content that you want to see (the show) four times for every time they'll show you what they want you to see, which is a commercial.

When marketing your business, you want to do the same thing. Give value 4x more than you ask for in return. This creates trust and reliability, and people only want to do business with people they like and trust.

Send your Target Market an interesting article. Write them an informative blog post. Teach them something new. Keep them engaged and truly help them out before you ask for the sale.

LUMPY MAIL

In 2009, I set out to acquire my first apartment building.

I got a list of every apartment owner in the San Fernando Valley, a highly populated area just north of Los Angeles.

I chose 500 building owners to target.

I purchased a box of stationary-type envelopes—the ones that look like they would have a birthday card from grandma in them—and I wrote a short letter and printed off 500 copies.

I also purchased a bag of little red and white mint candies.

I folded the short letter and stuffed a candy into each envelope I'd already addressed and stamped.

I then licked each envelope closed and dropped them all in the mailbox.

I got six calls from that mailer—all with buildings to sell.

I purchased my first building from that marketing campaign, and it cost me less than $300 to attract those motivated sellers.

I am sure I could have capitalized on every one of those six sellers that called me; but hey, I was still new at the game.

Marketing is the first step in becoming a DealMaker. Get motivated sellers to know you, so they will call you when they are motivated to sell.

PILLAR II:
SALES — THE LIFE-BLOOD
OF ANY ORGANIZATION

I was sweating bullets as I drove down the 405 Freeway. Twenty-four years old and on my way to meet with a top hedge fund owner.

Robin had plans drawn up to build his 5,000sf ocean view Los Angeles (weekend) pad in Bel Air.

The architect had referred me to bid on the project and by this time I had a thriving general contracting business. I knew Robin had taken bids from four contractors and had already eliminated two. In fact, he tried to eliminate me over the phone and I re-told him how hard I had worked on his bid and that I would not take no for an answer—at least until he allowed me to meet him in person one last time.

He agreed.

When I arrived at his office in Brentwood, he welcomed me in with a smug grin on his face, and I immediately opened the paperwork that made up my $3 million bid to build his house.

Robin cut to the chase: "The other guy in the running has 20 years' experience and has built homes like the one I have planned many times. You are young and inexperienced, and this would be your biggest project to date —why should I go with you?"

Good question...

I looked him square in the eye and responded with my well-rehearsed answer to the question: "Tom Brady is about to go to the Super Bowl. This is his second year in the NFL, and he barely played in college. Tom Brady is going to be the most prepared man on that field this Sunday because this is his big moment, his big show, and everyone knows he is going to want it more and will do whatever it takes to get the job done this weekend."

And I continued, "Your project is just another game for this other guy I'm bidding against, but for me, this is my Super Bowl. This is my big show, and I promise you that if you give me the opportunity to build your home, I will do whatever it takes to get the job done right because this is my shot."

We signed the contract that day. I sold it. I sold myself.

By the time I left Robin, he'd even said he was beginning to think of me as his little brother. It was a huge compliment from such an internationally successful guy. He gave me my start; opened the door for me to go on to build many more ultra-high-end luxury homes and I built a $9-million-dollar-a-year contracting business out of it in the roaring 2000's. I then parlayed the relationships I'd forged with these high-net-worth clients and turned them into investors in my development projects.

I've loved sales from a young age. As a kid, I would jump on my skateboard and cruise door-to-door offering to wash cars, cut lawns, and walk dogs for a few bucks. Throughout my life, sales was a constant. I delivered newspapers in grade school, sold magazines and candy bars for my high school football uniform and even sold snow ski equipment in Southern California one summer (and made a killing.)

Although it may seem as if these were simple jobs, these were some of the best experiences in my life. They taught me how to face rejection, overcome objections, and how to close. Most importantly, I learned what separates a good salesman from a great salesman. It's the simple realization that sales is wielding influence for a specific outcome and because of this, great salesmen are the most powerful people on the planet.

Sales is influence. A person who can sell has influence. They can cause things to happen. They hold a power in the mind, a power in the voice and tonality, and a power in speech patterns. This allows the salesperson to lead people and help them make wise decisions. This power can be used for good or ill intentions, no less; wielding leadership and influence is certainly a power.

Here's the good news. Salesmanship is not an inherent talent you have, or you don't have. It's a skill, like anything else, that is learned through practice and discipline. Salesmanship is the most powerful, highest paid skill set out there. A great salesman can make as much money as he'd like in his life because if you can sell anything, you can sell everything.

SALES DOCTOR

When done right, the sales process is a lot like being a medical doctor.

If you walked into a doctor's office and suddenly the doctor pounced on you and started telling you that kidney transplants were on sale and that you should buy one, you would run out of that office fast! Especially if you'd just gone in there for a simple cold remedy!

But people pretending to be in sales do this all the time. They pounce. They promote their crap to people who don't want or need it. Then they wonder why salespeople get a bad rap.

Just like a good doctor will take the time to listen to what's ailing his patient and then run tests to figure out what the problem is before he recommends a remedy, a great salesperson will listen twice as much as they speak. They will ask questions to fully understand their prospect's needs, wants, and pains. They will seek first to understand before being understood. And then the great salesperson will teach their prospect what how their service or product can help them solve their problem.

Always Be Prospecting

The first rule in Selling is generating prospects; you have to be in front of people that need and want what you're selling.

DealMakers will create a pool of hungry fish through attracting the right fish into their pool by chumming the water with great value-driven marketing content.

Prospecting then is separating the qualified from the unqualified.

The most valuable thing a salesperson can do is separate unqualified buyers as fast as possible. This is probably the most difficult thing the newest salespeople have to learn. They often hold out hope for far too long wishing an unqualified prospect (we call that a "suspect" in my office) will magically like them enough or that they will win the lottery and suddenly be able to afford what they're selling.

The Elevator Pitch

One tool that all great salespeople have in their toolbox is an elevator pitch. An elevator pitch is a speech that communicates exactly what you do and what's in it for "them" in the time it would take to ride an elevator one floor. Quick. To the point.

My A-Team (Acquisitions Team) use something like this:

"My name is Matt Skinner, and I buy apartment buildings in Arizona. I guarantee a full price offer within 24 hours. Are you interested in seeing a full price offer?"

I teach the fundraising sales team for my equity group an elevator pitch that goes like this:

"My name is Matt Skinner, and I lead a group of investors who buy value add apartment buildings in emerging US markets. We have a track record of delivering a higher rate of return to our investors than many people can typically find elsewhere. Are you investing in real estate?"

Notice that both elevator pitches cut to the chase and end with a question to engage the person we are speaking to.

These elevator pitches are usually preceded with a strategic "Nice to meet you, what do you do for a living?" And then the person will say what he or she does and almost 100 percent of the time respond in kind out of courtesy. These speeches are both designed to cull the crowd into prospect or not.

My team gets responses to their elevator pitch that range from: "Not yet, but I've always wanted to," to "I wish, I don't have any money," to "Yes, I've been investing for years, and I would like to know more about your program."

It works. Fast.

It's important to have your elevator pitch down, memorized, and ready to go whenever you have the opportunity to share what you do. I recommend you write your elevator pitch down, craft it, and then print it on a 3x5 note card and recite it a few dozen times each day until it flows naturally off your tongue without any thought required... like your phone number... and... always be prospecting.

Seek First to Understand Before Being Understood

Once you have a qualified prospect, you want to lead them through some strategic questions to find out what they are really looking for, what they need, and what their pain points are. If you skip this, you might end up trying to sell them something they don't want or need— and that's not good for either of you.

When we are selling an investment opportunity in our private equity fund I ask questions like:

- Have you ever invested in apartment buildings before?

- Have you ever invested with a group before?

- If you had a magic wand to create your perfect real estate deal, what would that look like?

- If I showed you the absolute perfect deal, how much available cash would you have to invest?

- Would your funds be coming from an investment account? Or your IRA or 401k?

- Are you looking for rapid growth or more of a stable stream of cash flow?

- What would you say your investment risk tolerance is?

And then I would use their answers to these questions to place them in the right opportunity (we do real estate development for a medium risk, short term, growth strategy and we buy value add apartment buildings for low-risk, long-term, growth and cash flow.)

KNOW THY PRODUCT

The one thing a great salesperson does is know their product and their competition. A great salesperson acts as an advisor and helps their client make the right decision. They know their product, their industry, their competitors (and their sins) inside and out. A great salesperson will leave their client knowing more than before the interaction.

ASK FOR THE CLOSE

So, you have qualified your prospect (are they able and willing to buy what you're selling?), you have learned where they're coming from by asking questions, and have thoroughly educated them about your product. Now, it's time to close.

Some of my favorites are:

The Either-or Close

"So, would you like to close escrow on the 10th or the 12th?"

The Assumptive Close

"I'm glad you like it. Will you be paying cash or will you be getting a loan?"

The "Let's Get the Paperwork Started" Close

"Great! I'll write that up right away and email you the paperwork for your approval."

You really only need one closing technique to be effective, but a great salesperson will have many in their toolbox.

There're tons of techniques to learn, and sales is a skill that develops through practice and repetition.

I've been training my in-house sales team every week on everything from marketing and prospecting, to closing for many years, and I train my DealMakers in our DealMaker Society that same way.

Pillar III:
Negotiation
– The Art of the Deal

Negotiation is truly an art, and a necessary one for you to master in order to become a great DealMaker.

Being able to negotiate will make you the most money in the shortest amount of time than any other skill you could possess.

Benjamin Franklin said, "A penny saved is a penny earned," and this is a true statement, especially when it comes to buying large ticket items like real estate. In real estate, you make your money when you buy, so every dollar you can shave off the purchase price is a dollar that drops straight to your bottom line. And when measured as a cash-on-cash return of investment, every dollar you do not have to put down increases your profit margin exponentially.

Imagine being able to make thirty, forty, or even hundreds of thousands of dollars from one phrase or one question asked... This is what you will do regularly when you master the art of negotiation.

The most powerful phrase I have learned to use in my career, and the one that has made me the most money in the shortest amount of time is this:

"If I paid cash and closed quickly what's the least you could take?"

This one question alone has made my investors and me hundreds of thousands of dollars in and of itself over the years.

So, when you first engage a Seller about buying their property, and they say they'd like to sell it for $400,000 — begin by asking that simple question:

"If I paid cash and closed quickly what's the least you could take?"

I've seen many, many Sellers drop their price as much as $40K, $50K, even a hundred thousand dollars right off the bat. Remember, by asking "if," you are not promising that you can or even will pay cash and close quickly, but by asking the hypothetical question it gets you to their ground zero a lot sooner.

RULES FOR NEGOTIATION

RULE #1: THIS IS NON-NEGOTIABLE

Probably the best negotiation gambit is to make the person you are negotiating with believe that whatever you are negotiating is "non-negotiable."

Have you ever asked for a discount at a store where the clerk said, "Oh, that's non-negotiable," or "We don't negotiate price," no, right?

This tactic works very well, especially when you are a Seller.

"Oh, you're interested in buying my building? I would have to get at least $3.2 million, or I wouldn't even be interested in discussing it."

Or, maybe we turn the tables around. You are the buyer looking to buy a house, and your Seller says they would like to pay $350,000. You might say, "Well the very best I could do would be $300,000, and I couldn't possibly move on that number whatsoever."

The number one way to get what you want is to make it seem up front that you don't have any room (or authority) to negotiate.

One property we purchased to develop was in Newport Harbor. Over a half acre of virgin (never developed) land on the water with a white sandy beach; it was the largest private dock on the whole Western seaboard. This property was prime.

We purchased it for $11.4M and immediately started getting offers to buy it from us, but we had every intention of subdividing it and building two 10,000 sf spec houses on it.

Every person inquiring about buying it or listing it for us we would tell that we couldn't possibly take a penny less than $20M.

Some people still made offers, but we held our position of "non-negotiable."

When the offer of $19M came in just a year after we purchased, we definitely took a second look. In fact, we are in escrow for that price as I write this book.

I don't think we would have gotten our purchase price up that high over what we'd paid if we'd started any of the conversations as a willing seller ready to make a deal.

I think this story also illustrates that just because someone you are negotiating with might say it's non-negotiable, it doesn't necessarily mean that's the last word.

RULE #2: ASK FOR MORE THAN YOU EXPECT TO GET

President Trump is a master of this gambit. In fact, as a lifelong student of his, I recognized something about his presidential campaign that was definately missed by everyone in the media. Donald Trump's entire campaign was an opening bid in what he considered a four-year negotiation.

It doesn't matter what your political persuasion is but many people have been calling for immigration reform, but he started his negotiation with demanding thousands of miles of wall. Now if he gets a more moderate comprehensive immigration reform bill passed he will have won something that no other politician was able to do.

He set the stakes much higher right from the beginning and rocked his opponents back on their heels.

If you are in a situation where you want to negotiate seller financing on a deal, and you know that you could get a loan, and you know that you could also afford to pay an interest rate of 7% or 8% to the get the deal done, you might be foolish to start your opening offer with the most you can give.

Instead, you might offer, "Well the only way I could do this deal at the price you are asking is if you carried financing for me." (Stating it this way uses DealMaker Rule #1: "Non-negotiable").

Once you have established that you will need seller financing to pay them their price and have made it appear that it is non-negotiable, next ask for a 4% rate instead of the 8% that you know you could pay if you had to.

Not only might you be surprised when they say yes, but it also leaves a little meat on the bone for you to concede something to them when they counter you at 6% and this will make your opponent feel they have won something, too.

RULE #3: NEVER SAY YES TO THE FIRST OFFER

Never ever say yes to the first offer. In fact, **always flinch.**

Sometimes a simple gasp of exasperation when you hear an opening price suggestion can change the landscape completely.

"That will be $100,000..."

"Whaaaaat? That's way too much."

"Well how about I give you 10% off?"

On one development project, one of my subcontractors called me to discuss a change order that he felt was necessary to be paid extra for. I had asked for a change in the plan, and he definitely deserved to receive something extra to perform the work outside the scope.

When the subcontractor called with his price of $22,000 I picked up a big book off my desk and dropped it on the floor causing an audible thud over the phone.

After a few hanging seconds of silence on the phone, my only response was "You've got to be kidding me."

The subcontractor immediately lowered his price by thousands of dollars because he'd heard the very contrived shock coming through my end of the phone.

Get in the habit of flinching whenever anyone gives you a price for anything, and you will be amazed at the discounts you will suddenly begin to realize on your bottom line.

RULE #4: Be the Reluctant Buyer/Seller

No matter if you are buying or selling, never act eager to do either.

When you are buying a property, never compliment the Seller on the property. In fact, remind them over and over again about all the things that are wrong with it and how difficult it will be to fix it all. You can psychologically devalue the property in their minds even before you've made your offer or entered into any kind of negotiation.

When you are selling a property, always play the reluctant seller, especially if you are desperate to get a deal done.

You might say things like, "Well, I was kind of thinking I might just keep this house I built and move into it." Or, "I was thinking this one might be nice in my portfolio as a rental."

Never come across as desperate. Hunters can sense blood in the water, and a good shark will take full advantage of this.

RULE #5: Higher Authority

This rule is one of my favorites.

Let's say you're deep in negotiation and you finally arrive at a price that you both agree could work.

Use this last negotiation gambit and really go in for the extra points.

So, you and your opponent agree on a purchase price on their building for $4.2million.

Your opponent is a good salesperson and uses the "Let's Get the Paperwork Done" close on you.

You say, "That will be great. Go ahead and draft the agreement and send it over to me." (This gets any seller psychologically and emotionally attached to the idea that they are moving forward with you) and then add, "But I will have to run this by my board of directors before I can sign it." You can use your wife, your banker, your partner— any higher authority you wish to utilize as the "Bad Cop" in your last bid in the negotiation.

When you get the agreement in your email, review everything and tell them whatever language issues you need changed and at the same time use the "Higher Authority" and "Good Cop/Bad Cop" strategy to nibble around the edges to get more of what you want or need.

You might say, "The deal looks really good, but my board of directors won't let me move forward on this unless we get an additional ten days of Due Diligence time." Or maybe you say, "Wow, this deal looks great to me, but my board of directors, they must be on a strange kick. They won't let us (yes, say "us"— it produces the perception that you and your opponent are on the same side working toward the same outcome) proceed unless they can see an additional $20,000 shaved off the purchase price." (Or the deposit amount, or whatever you think you can get at the last minute).

WARNING: Do not be a RE-TRADER.

No one likes a re-trader.

A re-trader is someone who makes a deal and then tries to renegotiate the deal that was made just before closing. This is the fastest way to get a bad reputation – especially in real estate.

All negotiation is fair game before a deal is made. But if you are going to nickel and dime your seller just before closing, people are going to hear about your tactic and not want to do business with you.

From time to time you may find out some new information about a property that could make it necessary to back out or re-trade. Just make sure you limit this to those extreme circumstances.

Don't BE a re-trader.

***

Negotiating is the single most valuable tool you will possess as a DealMaker, and it will make you more money than any other skill you can master.

When done right, you will make deals that are win-win and leave your opponent feeling great about working with you.

We spend a lot of time training very specific real estate-related negotiation skills in my DealMaker Society because DealMakers are killer negotiators who master the art of Making Deals and Getting Paid.

Pillar IV:
Management

Everybody gets the same amount of time each day. What you do with those 24 hours, how you manage your time, how you create systems that do things for you, and how you manage the people in your life will determine the amount of output you can accomplish in the same 24 hours everybody else has.

Time management is Life Management. It can be very easy to be pushed and pulled into doing things that don't serve your highest purpose. Ringing phones. Spammy email. Even a meaningless conversation around the water cooler can steal your most precious resource: your Life. Learn how to find your bigger "why" that will empower you to...

JUST SAY NO...

to the things (and people) in life that are not serving your best interest.

Systems are a series of things (or robots) that can do the same task over and over again, producing consistent results, so you don't have to do anything over and over again. Systems are tools that will allow you to free up more of your Life.

A car is a system. When it works properly, it will enable you to get from point A to point B in a consistent manner. Software is a system that can do tasks for you that need to be done, but that may not be the best use of your time.

Once you find a method of producing a positive result in your life, you need to systematize it so that that positive result will occur over and over again for you without much thought or effort.

When I found an effective way to use the correct messaging, the correct piece of mail, and the correct questions to answer when on calls, I created a system that enables me to produce highly motivated leads from people who have apartment buildings for sale. This lead generation system has enabled me to earn hundreds of thousands of dollars over the last several years with very little thought or effort (once the system was built) on my part.

Sometimes systems will involve people. But "the people" do not necessarily need to be you.

Ray Kroc, the founder of McDonald's, found a way to sell Billions of hamburgers without being there. He discovered the most efficient way of making the burgers, delivered them to thousands of stores, and created a system around what the store should look like, how to get customers inside, what the employees should wear, say, and do, and how to deliver the same burger with consistent and reliable results every time no matter where the restaurant was in the country, or around the world.

People also require management. When I owned and operated a $10-million-a-year construction company as a general contractor, my primary responsibility was to manage the people. We would find clients that needed something built, get the bids from the subcontractors that would do the work, and create the schedule and budget. Then we'd build the house or building according to the plans and specifications the architect and engineers gave us.

People would often question this method and ask, "Why do I need a general contractor?"

My response was always the same: "If plumbers, electricians, framers, tile setters and all of the other 56+ trades that it takes to construct a building would magically know what day to show up, would show up on time, do their best work without cutting corners, and work together in unity as a system, then you are right, someone may not need a general contractor for their project."

A DealMaker must master the three types of management skills to be able to BE, DO, and HAVE all the things he wants in life.

Time Management

I see so many people who are just pushed and pulled and go wherever pressures take them in their life. But they don't have any kind of management system for their life, for their time. Time is the number one most precious resource that any of us have as human beings.

Time in your life is important, and we only have so much time. So, how you use your time, how you spend your time or how you invest your time will radically change not only the outcome of your life but ultimately, it will also influence your joy and happiness.

Just like money, you can use money, you can spend money, but if you want it to grow, you need to invest money.

Same goes for time.

Invest your time and your life will grow.

I am on a plane from Hawaii to Los Angeles as I write this section. In front of me is a TV with a bunch of movies to watch on pay-per-view. And I love movies! But instead, I decide to use the five hours of travel to write this book. I could have chosen to watch a dumb action movie or the latest war movie instead...and these hours would have been wasted.

Invest your money.

Invest your time.

Happiness comes from overcoming obstacles. That's all happiness is. It's the feeling you get when you've beat a challenge. That's how true joy is created.

To experience true joy and happiness, the best thing you can do is set a course and go after it. Like the hiker who crests the peak of a mountain and feels joy at the work he's just accomplished. He enjoys the view and the amazing feat, and it's really important.

Time management is life management.

But the first thing you need to do to manage your life is to set the vision.

Where are you going?

What are you shooting for?

You can't hit a target that you can't see.

We set the target by designing your Perfect Day.

Design Your Perfect Day

I want you to spend some real time doing this exercise.

In your mind's eye, I want you to design your Perfect Day.

Start at the beginning of the day, and envision that Perfect Day minute by minute from the time you wake up to the time you go to sleep that night.

What does your Perfect Day look like?

What does it feel like?

What does it taste and even smell like?

Who will be there and where is "there"—where does your Perfect Day take place?

These questions have a real purpose behind them so think about them carefully.

What do you do after breakfast? Do you go to work? Is this in an office, or somewhere else? Maybe you work in a high-rise building; maybe it's from home.

Who is involved in your Perfect Day? Where will you have lunch and what type of food do you order?

Think in detail and take your time to go through this exercise.

By putting intention on your attention, you will begin to create in your mind this reality for yourself.

Your mind cannot distinguish the difference between what your eye sees and what your imagination sees. It just sees and then responds.

So, whatever you envision and begin to believe to be true, will be true for you because every electron in your body (yeah baby, you got atomic energy inside you— put it to work!!) will then be programmed to work toward the target you set for it.

The second you realize your mind is a powerful tool that commands the power of 7 billion, billion, billion (7×10^{27}) atoms and all the energy that is inside of each one of them, what could possibly hold you back?

NOW think about what your Perfect Day looks like.

Take a moment to sit down and really think it over.

Write it down. Be creative.

You get to write your own script.

The important thing to point out here is what I didn't say.

I didn't say:

What kind of car do you have?

How expensive is your house?

Is your watch $10,000 or $100,000?

These questions aren't as important. Sure, they can be part of your Perfect Day if you like. I'm just going to warn you; those may not be the things that will give you the Perfect Day you're truly looking for.

They certainly weren't for me.

Think about what is really important to you. Are you considering things such as people, or experiences, or the way you use your time? Probably, all three. But which are the most important? Include them all. I'm not saying don't consider what type of watch you're wearing, but just don't forget the kind of people you're with and the relationships you have. The way the people you surround yourself with make you feel and how you, in turn, impact their life is fundamental to a Perfect Day.

Real wealth is in who you get to BE, who you get to spend time with, and the kind of relationships you have.

Real wealth is in the freedom and opportunities you get to experience by being the best YOU that you can be.

TIME MANAGEMENT IS LIFE MANAGEMENT

Now that you've created your Perfect Day, you need to think about how and when you can achieve it. This is the time to break it down and create an Action Plan.

I want you to decide when that Perfect Day will happen for you. This might be six months from now, three years from now, five years from now. I would encourage you to have such lofty goals that it's going to take a little bit of time (and faith) to achieve them. You'll be more fulfilled and happier because of the struggle it took to get there.

Let's say for a second you set a goal that you're going to acquire 1,000 apartment units. You decide you can accomplish that in three years. You set your goal. You've decided when you want it done because a goal without a time frame is just a dream. You decide when that's going to be accomplished. Then you need to work backward.

Who do I need to BE?

What do I need to DO?

What do I need to HAVE in order to acquire 1,000 units three years from now? Then write those things down.

You're going to need investors.

You're going to need a good relationship with a lender.

You're going to need to have a marketing system to find great deals.

You have to have a great property management company.

You want to get all those things in place. Then chunk that down again and say, "Okay, in three years I have 1,000 units. I know that I need all these things. Where do I need to be one year from now to be on track for that 3-year plan? Where do I need to be in each quarter of this one year? Where am I going to be three months from now, six months from now, nine months from now, 12 months from now?

SET YOUR COURSE

What do you need to accomplish **this** month to be on track for your 3-year goal?

What do you need to do each week to be on track this week with your 1-month goal?

Then continue to reverse engineer that week down into a 7-day Action Plan.

Ask yourself *what do I need to do today, tomorrow, and the next day to be on track for my 3-year plan?*

If you plan your life like this, you will have a tremendous amount of success. You will be a successful person just from implementing this one tool.

HABIT

Every week, on Sunday night I sit down and write a list of all the things I need to do; all of them. I just go wild. I think about all the things I want to do, all things I need to do, all the things that are urgent, all the things that are not urgent but are still important. I write everything down, and I make a giant list. Then I say, "Okay. The first thing to do is go through and label things with a D. D stands for Delegate. What can I delegate and who can I delegate it to is the first round of business." I try to delegate everything I possibly can off that list.

That's also management. The people kind, and we'll get to that later in this chapter.

Somebody's going to manage your time, whether it's you choosing what's important to you and your Life Plan or somebody else delegating their Life Plan and action items to you.

I am fortunate. I have about 20 people who spend about a third of their life (eight hours a day) focused on my goals, not to mention all the affiliates and associates I have created around the country that are looking for deals, opportunities, and people that I want to attract.

Your time will be managed one way or the other, so decide who's going to manage your time and whose goals you are going to be working on, yours or somebody else's.

Each week make the list and delegate as much as possible. Then go back through and label all the most important things you need to do with an "A." All the "A" items, you have to get done this week. Some of them are urgent, and some of them are just important or not urgent, but you have to get them done to stay on track with your reverse engineered 3-year plan.

Immediately after labeling all your "A" items, get out your calendar and schedule them.

Then go through and prioritize the remaining list with B's and C's. The B items are things that I'd like to get done, but I don't have to, and C items will be gotten to if I ever finish my A and B list.

Truth is, I rarely do any C items. If the same items keep appearing on my list of C's every week, I either need to reevaluate their significance in my life, or I need to forget about them and get rid of them—which also is a form of time and life management.

By scheduling the most important things on your calendar, your life will be made up of only things that matter to you and your Life Plan.

I would encourage you to adopt this. I do it every Sunday night. It's a ritual. It's a habit.

Doing this has made me far more productive than most people I run into. I get compliments all the time like, "How do you get so much done?" That's my secret.

I use my calendar like a rule book, and it manages my life. And I manage my calendar BEFORE it's time to do things.

To stay on track, I use my birthday as a benchmark. Every year on my birthday, I go and spend time alone, and I think about where I'm at. I evaluate my previous year's goals, I evaluate my quarterly goals and use it as a reset button. This is just to make sure I'm on track and to make sure that I still want the 3 and 5-year goals I've written down.

As I progressively move forward day-by-day with every task that I've scheduled for myself, I'm constantly moving forward to the bigger vision of my life, the life I ultimately want to create. Once you reach that life, I promise you you'll be the kind of person who will reach further. You'll have bigger dreams and bigger goals. That's what we call Life Management. You get to design the life you want and then create it for yourself day-by-day, minute-by-minute, task-by-task each and every day.

Let me tell you; it's easy to say no to things that seem urgent but don't matter when you have a stronger yes to say yes to.

SYSTEMS MANAGEMENT

The next kind of management is called "systems and automation." When we talk about systems, it's a form of delegation. It's a way that you can automate a task that needs to be done over and over again. Once you've discovered the right or best way to do something it would be unwise to do it differently every time, and it would be equally unwise for you to do the same thing over and over again. I use systems to automate tasks, to make things easier in my life. Sometimes you might apply a manual system that you or an employee use to do the same process over and over again to get the same results. Some of the systems I would suggest that you get into, especially as a DealMaker are:

Email System: AWeber is a lifesaver. We have AWeber available in our toolbox for you. It's a great email management system where you can put all your contacts like that audience you're building in your marketing program. Put them all in there so you can email them all at the same time. One email, hundreds of people, maybe thousands.

Phone Scheduler System: MeetMe.so allows anyone to view my calendar and schedule a call with me **without** my involvement. You send the person a link and say, "Hey, pick a time on my calendar that would be good for you to talk." They just look at your calendar; they don't see anything else other than the open times that are available. They get to pick a time, 15-minute slot, 20-minute slot, 30-minute slot, whatever you decide is a sufficient amount time. They tell you what the call is going to be about. They are just able to schedule their own appointments.

Direct Mail System: Automatically send information to your list of leads. Whether they're sellers, buyers, or investors, you're going to need something that keeps you in constant contact with your audience. Make sure you develop a system like that. I recommend Click2Mail. It's an automated postcard mailing system where we design the postcard. We just load it up onto their software, then I put in my list of leads and set it on autopilot. It emails every Tuesday or the same day every month, very consistent. I don't even have to think about it. My people are getting contacted by me regularly. This constant communication is useful, so I really recommend setting up this system to benefit you.

Client Relationship Management System [CRM]: You need to remember all the people you've talked to, where they're at, and where you left off... And who has dogs, and who likes to golf, and sail, and who each contact is and you have to take notes, and keep tabs and maintain a system, so you don't forget you have a hot client who wants to buy your stuff, and then you space calling them. You need a system that helps you to be more successful and more productive.

An Accounting System: Everything that you do should go into an automated system. Get a robot to do the work for you, so you don't have to do these things over and over again. You can focus your time on making deals and getting paid.

PEOPLE MANAGEMENT

All business is about people, whether you're in real estate or tech or any other industry; it's all about people.

When you are a leader – and you are now that you are a DealMaker – your number one job on this planet is to develop people.

The best way to manage people is to give them a vision of what a good job looks like; show them what successful behavior will look like. Give them the tools and best practices for being efficient to do that good job you described. Then get out of the way. This is true for employees, salespeople, even customers. Think about it; what if you taught your customer how to be a good customer?

The key to managing people well is understanding how to motivate and how to wield power well. Yes, I said power.

"Power" these days can sound like a dirty word. But...

Power is the ability to reward and reprimand.

The degree to which you can reward and/or reprimand another person is the degree to which you have the power to influence them.

If you were given the task of managing a football team but had no power to make them run sprint laps, do extra push-ups or stay late after practice, you would wield no influence over them. Conversely, if you also had no say on who started in the games or who had playing time, you would have no power to reward either. So, why would anyone do anything you said?

Have you ever seen a player on the field change up his performance because of what some loud drunk guy was yelling from the stands? Drunk guys in the stands have no power... No influence. No matter how much they might think they do.

I'll tell you, my football coaches had the most power over my life and were the most influential people in my life (at that time) because I wanted to start, and I never wanted to run extra sprint laps.

You can't manage what you do not measure, so it's important to track the performance of any person you are managing and measure if they are getting better at their job, getting more efficient, and taking on more responsibility.

Make sure you reward good behavior as often as possible and do it immediately and in public whenever possible.

Make sure you also reprimand bad behavior and try to avoid doing that in public as often as possible.

Give the people you are managing a clear picture of what a great job would look like, and what a poor job would look like. Give them as much information and as many tools to do the job to the best of their ability; then measure their progress. Be sure to reward and reprimand as they go so they can be guided and will grow in the right direction.

Pillar V:
Financial Intelligence

Buy Low. Sell High.

Buy Low. Sell High. Sounds like the most ridiculously obvious advice, doesn't it? I actually tried it the other way around once, and it didn't work out so well.

Many people who call themselves "investors" do it the opposite way every single day (and thank God that they do, because that's exactly the kind of Seller I am looking for.)

People hear a hot stock tip that a stock is going up, and then they rush out to buy it! But it's too late. The stock has already risen. They bought high. And when the value drops they will say, "Oh no! I better get out before it goes any lower!"

People do the same thing in real estate.

In 2010, I lead a team of investors (and our money) from California to Texas to buy apartment buildings. At the time, Texas was the only state creating jobs and businesses were fleeing from other states to seek refuge in the business-friendly, low-overhead, low-tax, environment of Texas.

Convincing Californians when real estate values were crashing all around them to buy something, especially in another state, was the hardest sales job I had to do.

But it paid off.

I saw Texas as the last beacon of hope during the great recession of 2008. I studied the migration of businesses and watched as Governor Perry ran ads in other states inviting companies to come to Texas. And I went there early and bought up apartments just as the demand began to explode.

This is called contrarian investing.

Texas had at that time what I call a perfect storm.

Businesses were relocating there and creating jobs.

People were losing their homes all over the country and seeking new opportunities, a fresh start; so, they came to Texas in search of those new jobs.

The demand for housing was swelling as more and more people moved there.

But in 2010 no banks were giving loans— especially not construction loans—so no new housing supply was being created.

There was a rising demand with no way of creating new supply.

This was the perfect recipe to buy as the demand overwhelmed the supply causing prices to begin to rise as people competed for apartments.

Four years later, I continued to watch the market indicators. In 2014, over 22,000 new permits were being issued in Dallas to construct new apartment buildings to meet the overwhelming demand for housing that had been created.

Builders were stepping up to the plate to create new supply.

It was then that I knew we needed to get out.

In the years following, demand has slowed in Dallas (the great business migration is pretty much done), and the supply of housing is being met with great gusto, leveling out the huge momentum in the marketplace. There's construction going on all over the place there.

Today, when I hear real estate entrepreneurs sing the praises of going to Texas to invest I think about telling them they are nearly a decade too late.

As I write this book, Texas apartment buildings are enjoying their lowest vacancy rates, their lowest cap rates, and their highest price-point per unit the Texas multifamily market has ever seen.

Not a good time to buy.

Remember: Buy low. Sell high.

Conversely, Arizona is still at the bottom of its recovery cycle. In 2014 when I first started buying that target market we could barely get a loan because banks were still scared of that tertiary market.

What I knew then, and we are seeing happen now, is there was about to be a tech boom in Arizona.

Startup companies go to Silicon Valley and Silicon Beach (Santa Monica) and get their seed round money from Angel Investors and Venture Capital groups. They then immediately move to Arizona where they have a business-friendly environment, low taxes, cheap land and wages to operate their business.

Apple is building a $2-billion data center there.

Intel has moved its major operations there.

State Farm Insurance recently moved their headquarters there and are building high-rise office buildings.

Call centers are popping up all over.

And Scottsdale has welcomed this economic phenomenon by building huge tech park campuses like those you would see in Cupertino California.

MARKET CYCLES

All markets cycle. They go up. They go down. Supply and demand ebbs and flows and so do the assets in those markets.

In the stock market, a single company can go through an entire market cycle in a matter of hours and be completely manipulated by emotions of the stock exchange or a wily hedge fund running their famous pump-and-dump strategy.

Real estate market cycles usually take years to complete. They don't turn on a dime like other equities markets and are not subject to the whims of a few manipulators like the stock market is. This is what makes real estate safe...or at least safer.

This makes it relatively easy to predict and follow for someone like me who makes it my business to know the local market trends, and I can easily play the market and buy before the market emerges and exit before it corrects.

We look for strong indicators in a market before we enter it. I look for strong signs of a city that is about to grow—or emerge. Some indicators are job growth, business-friendly government, low regulation, specialized resources, and major infrastructure that can support the growth.

Cities that have these indicators we call "emerging markets." Every city in the US has an Economic Development Plan which is where the local governmental leaders lay out their strategy to increase tax revenue. Government can only increase tax revenue by taxing its people more or by attracting businesses and creating incentives for more people and more businesses to move there.

YOUR INCOME IS IN DIRECT PROPORTION TO THE VALUE YOU GIVE THE WORLD

It took me many years to figure this out.

LeBron James is the highest paid NBA player because no one in the world can do what he does.

Apple became one of the largest companies on the planet because they impacted billions of people's lives with their devices in a way that no one before ever had. Steve Jobs called the personal computer the "bicycle for the mind" because it exponentially made humans more efficient.

I earned very little money as a ditch digger because just about anyone could offer the same value that I offered at that time.

But when I discovered how to create deals that no one else could, when I began to organize capital in a way that limited my investors' risk and maximized their returns, when I began to demonstrate I could consistently give my investors a higher rate of return than they could typically find elsewhere, that's when I began to provide a unique value that many other people could not replicate or compete against.

Figure out what you can give the world that no one else can, and your value will be invaluable; your income and net worth will reflect your invaluableness.

If you don't like how much you're making now, find a way to increase the amount of value you're giving, and the money will come. It just has to. It's a universal law.

The more value you give to the world the more resources will come to you.

Money is Just a Measurement of Resources

Back in the day, a person who was wealthy had land, cattle, crops, children, and so on. These were all resources that made a wealthy man's life easier. Today, we just use money as an exchange instead of trading cows.

Start to look at money as a resource that enables you to have more choices, and you'll add more value to the world around you.

The more unique value you give to the world the more resources the world will give you; it's a different mindset than chasing a paycheck.

Specialize

Don't be a jack of all trades. Specialize. Find the one thing that you love and that you are uniquely qualified to give to the world and then be the best at it.

I have hundreds of investors that have invested with us. Ninety-five percent of them reinvest their money with us into the next project because we do such a terrific job. We give them the returns that they're looking for, I do what I say I'm going to do. I finish projects on time, and on a budget. People want to reinvest in a system like that because we specialize. We are better at this than anyone else out there.

Always Add Value

As a kid, my dad taught me always to leave things better than I found them.

I later learned that applied to people, too.

But the number one thing I like about real estate investing is that I am uniquely qualified as a builder, a contractor, and as a great manager of systems and people, to quickly add value to a property.

In the early years of my real estate investing career, I would buy houses and fix them up for resale. This was a great start for me—especially with my skill as a contractor.

But even for a contractor, this strategy is probably one of the highest risk methods to invest in because you never know what you will find when buying an old piece of junk house.

To balance out this high-stakes game of fixing and flipping houses and add a little cash flow to my life, I would then use some of the profits I'd earned from fix and flips and buy rental houses. This is the equivalent of buying a job after weighing in the time and effort it takes to manage one house as a rental.

Recent reality shows (which are complete bullshit), have made flipping houses sexy so now everyone and their mother are trying to do it. With the influx of buyers of a limited resource, the entry price to fixing junker houses has risen with the demand, and it is extremely difficult to get a good deal.

After fixing and flipping houses for a few years, I decided I would promote myself and graduate.

I began doing real estate development projects which are far less risky than buying junker houses and far more profitable. I compete in the space of multimillion dollar homes where my buyers have cash. I don't have a lot of competition, and my houses sell fast because there's less supply than there is demand. We are able to make a sizable profit on development projects in a reasonable amount of time with a very low or mitigated risk.

Next, I added apartments to my Firm's portfolio because of their low risk, stable, dependable nature.

When the market crashed in 2008, I saw all my house flipper friends go bust. I also saw all my friends who owned apartment buildings thriving through the recession. It was then that I realized I wanted to be "that guy" and will always buy apartment buildings, add value, and keep them for long-term cash flow, tax benefits, growth, a hedge against inflation, and safety.

Even institutions like pension funds, life insurance funds, and other financial institutions buy apartments because they believe they cannot lose money by owning them.

I graduated from house flipper and landlord to real estate developer and apartment building owner, and I believe everyone should use these unique strategies to their advantage.

Larger deals, in general, have less risk than smaller deals. Larger deals get better financing from banks and are more attractive to smart investors because of this.

RULE OF 72

The **Rule of 72** is a simplified way to determine how long an investment will take to double, given a fixed annual rate of return. Dividing **72** by the annual rate of return will give investors the number of years it will take for the initial investment to double. So, if your annual rate of return were 6%, your investment would double in 12 years.

My Freedom Fund, which owns and operates apartment buildings, has an annual return of 15% or better so my investors can reasonably expect for their investment to double in about six years.

My development projects return 25% or more annually to the investors so they can expect to double their money in about four years.

Compound Interest

Compound interest (or compounding interest) is interest calculated on the initial principal and the accumulated interest of previous periods of a deposit or loan.

You can find a compound interest calculator on my DealMaker app by texting DealMaker to 21000.

Compound Equity

Here's what investors like. Compound equity is calculated on the initial principal investment (equity) and the accumulated profit of previous projects.

For example, if you invest in a real estate development deal using a tax-deferred IRA, you can compound the rate of growth on your equity.

So, if you invested $100,000 in a development project with me and earned a 25% annual return (for two years), you would get $150,000 after two years. Then you reinvest that new principal capital balance into the next development project tax deferred and earn a 25% annual return on $150,000 bringing your Compounded Equity to $225,000 over four years, which is more than double.

A Roth IRA works even better because taxes are not deferred; you are investing post-tax dollars and will never have to pay taxes on those profits.

RISK VS. REWARD

In order to do big deals and fulfill your big ideas, you have to be a DealMaker. To be a DealMaker, you don't have to take big risks, contrary to what a lot of people seem to think.

I'll tell you right now, I am very risk-averse.

Remember that course I told you I'd invested heavily in earlier? It was a risk. But I had to make it work. The risk I took was so great that I simply had to make it work. Otherwise, I wouldn't have been able to pay off that credit card debt. At least, it would have taken me an extremely long time to do that with the wages I was earning at the time.

I do big deals, and I look at dozens of deals before I green-light even one of them. I do this with a lot of thorough diligence. I scour the market. I know the market. I know the activities. I know the political climate in the area. I know the players before I even go in and make the deal. This is called a calculated risk.

There's a thing we say in the office when making deals: nothing is true unless it can be proven in three ways. Just because a broker or seller says the rent is one thing, I still want it to be proven. I want to see it on a lease. I want to see it on a check stub. I want to see it on a tax return. I want to see three ways before I believe it is true. Once it's been proven three ways, then I can believe it.

This is a reasonable way to verify it and how I do my due diligence on any property before I buy it.

So, when I do find a deal, it is 100% green-lighted. And by the time my investors hear about a deal from me, I've scoured the due diligence.

Doing thorough due diligence mitigates a lot of risk. You need to confirm what you know and find out what you don't know.

Operating under the philosophy that you make money when you buy (not when you sell) mitigates risk. When you buy properties, if you could sell it immediately for more money you are investing. If you are buying assets and hoping they will go up in value, you are gambling.

I never gamble.

I just did land a deal last year. I bought four-acre parcels for $225,000 per acre. Comps in the market showed similar properties had sold for $550,000. I knew that on day-one when I closed, I had made money. That's what I call "making money you buy."

I purchased an apartment building a couple of years ago in Arizona for $1.8 million. It had a current market value of well over $2 million. I estimated I could probably flip it for $2.2 million on the day I purchased it. We operated it for a few years and actually just sold it and made much, much more than that $2.2 million. In fact, it sold for $2.8million — a million more than my purchase price.

My investors and I made money when we bought. Everything else over that is just gravy.

One property I bought in Dallas was a $5 million asset. Based on its current income and expenses, current cap rate, I bought it for very little money down and took over $3.7 million debt using Creative Financing. We'll talk about using creative financing and leverage in the DealMaker Fulcrum section in a later chapter, but for now, I want to point something out. I'm not talking about just going out and throwing out low-ball offers hoping someone will accept them. It's very, very rare to get a bunch of equity for no particular reason.

A DealMaker is a problem solver. Solving problems, and doing it well, will get you fantastic deals. Great deals are made, not found. You're not going to walk down the street and just stumble across a great deal. You won't find one by popping open MLS (Multiple Listings Service.) If you're going to create a career in real estate, then you need to make a habit of doing great deals. You need to know how to create deals, not just find deals, and when you can do that, you'll be a DealMaker.

WHAT YOU NEED TO KNOW ABOUT CAPITALIZATION RATES

Capitalization rates, or Cap Rates, is a figure used to compare two like and kind income properties—usually apartments or commercial buildings.

The Cap Rate is figured by taking gross annual income and subtracting the operating expenses for the same period. The result is the NOI (Net Operating Income.)

If you divide the NOI by the purchase price, this will give you the Cap Rate.

Cap Rate = NOI/Price

If you take the NOI and divide it by the Cap Rate, this will give you the current market value.

Value = NOI/Cap Rate

Capitalization Rate literally means a measure of time: How long will it take you to capitalize or put your principal investment back into your pocket?

So, if you purchased a property for $1 million and the cap rate was 6 (.06%) if you paid cash for the asset, 6% of your purchase price— $60,000—would be returned to you each year— or capitalized.

Cap Rates are to multifamily as "comps" are to the single-family world. They are only relevant if you are comparing two like-and-kind properties and they allow you to compare like-and-kind assets that have a different number of units and ensure you pay a premium for good management and get a discount for poor management.

Cap rate is a way to measure the sales price of two comparable properties, but many people misconstrue the story that a cap rate tells.

I hear a lot of people say, "I only buy ten cap properties anywhere in the US." Hmmm...

That would be the same as someone saying, "I only buy $400,000 properties anywhere in the US."

A $400,000 property in Beverly Hills would most likely be a steal. But a $400,000 house in other markets in the US would be way too high of a price for any asset. This misconception can even happen across the railroad tracks in the same city.

For example, in Los Angeles, a 6 cap in The Valley (San Fernando Valley is one of the highest demand rental markets in the US) would be a great deal. But a 6 cap in more rural areas in Ohio or Kansas City—where apartments compete with houses—would be super expensive.

Ultimately, a cap rate is a measure of risk. Markets that have strong demand for occupancy have a very low cap rate. Markets that have a very low demand for occupancy and therefore are more difficult to manage, have a higher cap rate.

San Francisco, Manhattan, San Fernando Valley, and other major cities typically have low cap rates because the demand for apartment housing remains strong through any market cycle.

Tertiary markets in smaller towns in Texas or Ohio have higher cap rates because the demand for rental housing is not as strong, making the risk factor much higher.

The proper way to use cap rates is relative to their location. When you go into a new market, find out what cap rate similar properties are selling for (price will vary depending on the number of units.) If you find that a 6 cap is market rate price for the type of asset you are contemplating, then buying at a 5.5 is paying too much. Conversely, buying at a 6.5 might be a great deal.

The higher the cap rate, the riskier the deal. The lower the cap rate, the less risk.

Now that you know one way to assess risk lets dive into the first steps of creative real estate financing; the DealMaker Fulcrum.

DealMaker Fulcrum

A fulcrum is a pivot point where a lever rests.

A teeter-totter or a seesaw is a lever and a fulcrum; it has an apex or pivot point in the middle and a lever on both sides. As the weight is distributed on one side, that lever raises up on the other side. As the weight is distributed more heavily on the other side, the other side begins to rise.

DealMaking is very similar to this analogy in the sense that every deal, every buying opportunity has a

DealMaker Fulcrum. On one side of the fulcrum is PRICE and on the other side of the fulcrum is TERMS.

Price is how much a buyer is willing to pay.

Terms are the circumstances under which you would be willing to buy.

Real estate agents are trained to find the most balanced price and terms; a reasonable price with reasonable terms equals a smooth retail transaction.

If you are chasing commissions, then you will probably want to shoot for balanced transactions with zero hiccups, too.

But if you're a DealMaker and an investor you are going to want to radically UNBALANCE the DealMaker Fulcrum.

Oftentimes, you can pay very little for a property if you pay all cash and close quickly, when that meets the seller's needs.

Other times you may agree to pay more than retail pricing if the seller is willing to give you terms you want; like zero down payment or low monthly payments that allow you to get into a property with very little money and make a large cash-on-cash return.

Rarely, will you be able to get both a great price and great terms but as a DealMaker, you will find a balance driven by what the seller's needs or motives are for selling.

Many would-be real estate entrepreneurs are taught just to shoot out "low-ball" offers.

You go to a seller and say, "I'll give you all cash and close quickly." And sometimes this will work. However, this method is flawed. You haven't properly diagnosed the situation on what your seller needs. You might be making an offer that's ridiculous.

Let's say you have a seller who thinks his house is worth $500,000; you might say, "Hey I'll give you all cash and close quickly, and I'll give you $400,000 for the property." He could say, "Get the hell out of my house." It's insulting. The price is ridiculous. You've just learned that your seller couldn't care less about being paid cash and closing quickly.

Now, on the other hand of the DealMaker Fulcrum, a lot of would-be real estate entrepreneurs get stuck because they say, "Well, I made the offer and... you know, I can't pay full retail." They only have half a toolbox. Offering all cash with a quick close is offering terms that you think the seller wants but you need to dig and find out what they really need.

Like a doctor, you need to first diagnose your patient — then prescribe the solution.

Being a DealMaker is a lot like being a kung fu master. In kung fu, they teach you how to use your opponent's movements and energy against them. As a DealMaker, you want to seek first to understand what your seller wants and needs, and have them tell you anything and everything about them; then you can diagnose the seller's situation and figure out a way to give them what they need.

IRS Lady: Your Terms My Price

A while ago, I had a seller who called me from a Facebook ad I had done, and she said, "Look, your ad said you'd pay cash and close quickly. I have an IRS tax bill that's due a week from Tuesday. If I don't close before then, they're going to seize all my assets and freeze my bank accounts, and I'm planning to travel to Israel during that period, so that would be really difficult for me." Difficult. No kidding.

I don't know the full extent of her situation, but she felt like there was a big need to be able to sell a property and pay off her IRS bill, which sounded like the right thing to do.

I quickly diagnosed she wasn't too interested in the price tag she was getting. Of course, she needed to get enough money to pay off her bill, but she was more interested in getting that quick close, so she didn't lose everything.

I looked at the deal, did my due diligence and we paid her cash and closed quickly at a great price. I gave her the terms she wanted (Her Terms: Quick Close), and she gave me my price (My Price: Deep Discount). That's how the DealMaker Fulcrum works.

DALLAS DIVORCE: YOUR PRICE MY TERMS

In another circumstance, I did a deal in Dallas with a seller who had about 200 units. They were going through a divorce and had been ordered by the divorce court to sell their apartment building and use the proceeds to pay off some joint debts and to settle the divorce.

This asset was worth about $5 million. They had a loan for about $3.7 million. On paper, they had $1.3 million in equity. The judge saw that and ordered, "Okay, sell the property, and we'll split that up to pay off your debts."

However, the problem was the bank. The lender had given them a very severe prepayment penalty, so if they sold the property before a certain time, the seller would have to essentially pay all the interest the lender would have earned during the entire length of the loan. This type of prepayment structure is called "Yield Maintenance Fee" and is fairly common on large balance loans because the bank could lose money putting out millions for short periods of time at a low interest. After all, there is a cost associated with organizing and placing capital, even for banks.

The bank stance in this situation was a lot like Uncle Paulie's famous line in *Goodfellas*: "Fuck you, pay me." According to the terms of the loan, the bank would get nearly $1 million dollars in yield maintenance for an early pay-off. And my seller was forced to sell.

It didn't take a rocket scientist to realize that with $1 million in Yield Maintenance Fees, closing costs, and a broker fee their $1.3 million was all but gone— and that's IF they were able to sell the asset at full retail price. They would have had no money to split up had they done it that way. In typical government fashion, they tried fixing one problem by creating another one.

DealMakers don't do that.

I put on my problem-solving hat. For some reason, this loan also was not assumable, so that solution was out. I could have taken the property "Subject To" taking the deed subject to the existing encumbrances, but I would have run the risk of the bank finding out and foreclosing, exercising their Due on Sale Clause. Although I have never actually heard of that happening, a million dollars is a lot to gamble in that type of "what-if."

So, here's what I did.

The seller owned the property in a trust with no other assets. I spent many hours reading his loan documents and his trust agreement and then came up with the solution.

My solution provided the Sellers more than they could otherwise expect to get (Their Price) and I got some decent Seller financing (My Terms).

I paid the seller half of what he thought he had in equity or about $600,000 (discount!) in exchange for 49%

ownership in their trust; 49% would not trigger the due-on-sale clause.

Then I directed the seller's attorney to modify the trust, so there were five trustee seats; the sellers were both still in the trust as guarantors of the loan, but I stacked the board with three additional seats giving my two appointed trustees and me full control.

I also got an exclusive right to buy them out of the trust or buy the property for $1 if and when the loan's Yield Maintenance fee burned off.

On paper, the sellers were 51% owners, which satisfied the lender.

Affectively I was in full control – even to the point of getting rid of the Sellers whenever I wanted them out of the deal.

I ran all that through the lawyers and got it approved by the lender. Because we followed their guidelines to the tee, they had to accept it. I found the loopholes to get through, and we got it approved by Fannie Mae.

This was another DealMaker win-win-win situation.

The sellers got $600,000 more than they would have gotten if they'd sold to someone else.

The bank got to keep their loan in place and collect the interest they wanted.

I got $700,000 off a great asset (discount) with $3.7 million in low-interest long-term seller financing and paid minimal closing costs.

I delivered a solution through creative real estate terms, and that earned my investors and me nearly $1 million in value.

THE IMPUDENT GRANDSON

One time I got this call from a woman who wanted to sell her house. She was elderly and had purchased a house in Los Angeles and then rented it to her grandson. Her grandson made the first month's rent, then moved his girlfriend in and never paid rent again.

Grandma was stuck paying the mortgage while her young, able-bodied grandson and his girlfriend lived rent free on grandma's dime.

By the time she had called me, this had gone on for over a year.

She practically begged me to buy her house from her. She said she just didn't have the heart to evict her grandson and didn't want to face him at Thanksgiving dinner in a few weeks after evicting him.

She said she would give me the house if I would take over the payments on her mortgage if I agreed to evict her grandson and keep her out of it.

I agreed. I like free houses.

It took me no time at all to evict them, and grandma had a drama-free Thanksgiving.

I got a free house (with a boatload of equity), and hopefully, grandson got the opportunity to learn to take care of himself like a man.

When you follow my systems, you will be amazed at how many free houses come your way.

***

The DealMaker Fulcrum shows us there are more ways to skin the cat than just offering a low price and hoping a seller will take it.

We go into all kinds of creative real estate financing in our DealMaker Academy program called Creative Real Estate Financing. We talk about leases. We talk about options. We talk about leases with options. We talk about master lease options. We talk about "Subject To," all-inclusive trust deeds, seller financing, seller carry-back, wraparound mortgages; all these different creative financing techniques that go on in the real estate world. I even give you all the documents you need to execute them.

If you don't know what any one of those terms mean, then you need to run to get involved in this Academy training because it will open up your ability to Make Deals and Get Paid like never before.

THE NUMBERS TELL A STORY

A major part of financial intelligence is knowing how to read financial statements. This is a key component especially as you get into larger deals with development and commercial income property like apartments.

A financial statement tells you a story about how a business or a building has operated over time. It tells you if there were problems during certain points of the year. It tells you if there were leasing issues during certain points of the year. Maybe you look at a financial statement, and you can see what the weather is like in that particular area. For example, Arizona electricity bills always go up like crazy during the summer because they have to run air conditioners all the time. I can tell what kind of weather they had just by reading financial statements. You will be able to do this, too.

A friend of mine bought an apartment building a few years back. Like me, she was well-versed in reading financial statements, and because she was so well-versed in her market and making deals, she knew how much a water bill should cost per unit in her Target Market. When she was looking at a certain property, she said, "Oh my gosh, there's something going on with their water bill. It's outrageous...two or three times more than what it ought to be for that size building."

As soon as they got into escrow and had started their due diligence, the story the financial statement told her led her to ask the right questions. What she discovered was a water leak underground in the main.

The seller was just paying for water that was seeping into the ground. My friend discovered a major water leak simply through reading the financial statements! She was able to identify the problem and fix the problem. It saved her thousands of dollars in water bills every year and increased the value of her property because she fixed that pipe. She made a lot of money all because she knew how to read a financial statement.

In Dealmaker Society, I teach you how to read financial statements, specifically pertaining to apartment buildings. You need to know how to read the rent roll and discover how the financials really tell the story. It's not just about dollars and cents or the numbers. It's about learning the ebbs and flows of the market and the ebbs and flows of that particular asset.

KNOW A GREAT DEAL WHEN YOU SEE ONE

Another part of financial intelligence is knowing how to spot a good deal. You know people who find stuff at a flea market for 100 bucks, and they're like, "This is worth $300 if I sell it on eBay," and they make good money doing that. I know quite a few people who are in that kind of business, and they do well. That's another form of financial intelligence. Knowing your market, knowing what other people are willing to pay; it's a skill you can develop, and that will lead to your financial intelligence.

When investing, always try to put as little down or as little in as possible and get as much out as possible.

When buying apartment buildings, the less you put down, the more money you can make using leverage and good financing.

One example of this was when I took over an existing loan on my very first apartment building. In this case, I took over the payments "Subject To," and I gave the seller a small down payment. I had the seller carry the balance of the down payment. By doing that, I only invested a couple hundred thousand dollars as a down payment, and I was able to take what probably would have been a cash flow of 5% if I'd purchased it traditionally. I turned it into a 13% cash-on-cash return by structuring the deal to put as little down as possible.

The less money you put in, the less risk you have in the asset. The risk is eliminated when you get your principal out of the deal and back into your pocket as fast as possible.

MAKE MONEY WHEN YOU BUY

If you don't make money when you buy, you are just gambling.

When you buy an apartment building, you have bought a system. You've bought an operation that hopefully throws off some cash flow and hopefully goes up in value. If you buy an asset you can sell immediately—and that's the only kinds of deals we like to do, where we know the value of what we're getting is higher than the dollars we're putting in—then you're not a gambler. You are a savvy investor. When you're able to do that, you are the essence of Dealmaker.

ANCIENT WISDOM

I was in escrow to buy a 150-unit apartment building in Texas, and I needed more time to close because my loan wasn't ready.

That scenario was common at that time because loans were hard to come by during the great recession. Back then, loans were tough to get even for apartment buildings, which are usually the most stable and the easiest loans to put together.

I flew from California to Texas just to meet with my seller about extending our closing date because of the bank. I offered to release some money from escrow in exchange for an extra 45 days on my escrow so that my loan could close.

I knew he was friends with George H.W. Bush. He played golf with him often. He was a big contributor to the Republican Party. He owned thousands and thousands of units in Texas. He was a developer who built lots of buildings. I knew he was a very wealthy man. When I got to his office building (I already knew he owned it), it looked like a normal C-class type of building. I was surprised. So, I went up to his office and walked in. He had a secretary; old desks that seemed to have been purchased in the 80's and piles of paper everywhere. Just to be very clear: he was active, and this office was also very active.

I sat down with him, and we made a deal. Probably one of the greatest negotiations I've done because it saved a smart deal at no cost to my investor group or me. I had already written up my proposal, and I passed it across the table for him to sign. He pulled out a pen that didn't write and threw it in the trash. Then he pulled out another pen, and that one didn't write either. So, he pulled out *another* pen. I could see him getting frustrated at this point. He looked at me with penetrating eyes and said:

"As you can see, we don't spend a lot of money on overhead. We invest our money into deals that make a good return."

I laughed out loud.

I know he said what he did because he was kind of embarrassed, but that lesson stuck with me about how he didn't invest in a fancy office; he didn't spend money on designer pens or even office materials. Rather, he took all his dollars, and he was a self-made man, and he invested all his dollars back into deals that gave him a good return. I admire that. I think there's nothing wrong with having a nice car, nice building, a nice house, nothing wrong with making money whatsoever. However,

I learned a very important lesson from that man that day, and it has stayed with me ever since.

Having financial intelligence is a skill set you can develop. As you go forward in your career, it's very important, especially as an investor; you must have the ability and skill set of financial intelligence.

Make Deals – Get Paid

Getting Started

Many people like to start their real estate career flipping houses. They see the reality TV shows, or they hear a guru teach a class on flipping houses, and they set out into the world to flip houses. Sexy.

But buying junker houses, fixing them up, and then selling them, can be risky business (that's why they have to pay a healthy profit margin) especially if you don't have the real estate, construction, interior design, management and marketing experience of a trained professional.

Truth is, you can get started in any category of real estate investing if you master the Five Pillars. As you master the Five Pillars, all you need is to have a clear strategy to Make Deals and Get Paid.

My A-Team (Acquisitions Team)

Over the last seven years, I have had the pleasure of coaching, teaching and training my A-Team. These guys and gals are highly-trained real estate entrepreneurs who I have personally taught how to be DealMakers. Their job is to make deals for my investment firm.

It started in the depths of the recession. I recruited a bunch of would-be real estate entrepreneurs to make hundreds of offers on REO (bank owned) properties. We would just write low-ball offers on everything that hit the market and the ones that were accepted (about 1 in 20) we wholesaled to rehabbers.

Over the years, my A-Team has evolved, and now I have land hunters for development, apartment hunters for value add apartment deals, and a special group that goes after pre-foreclosures or Delta deals.

Every week, I train my A-Team on the Five Pillars and in real estate techniques.

THE DEALMAKER CHECK DOWN SYSTEM

Every single seller that responds to your marketing should be paying you. We call this the "check-down system."

The "Check Down" is a football term. When a quarterback like Brady drops back to pass he's got his number one target, he knows who he's going to throw it to first, if he's open.

That's his first check-down.

If the guys covered he can check down to his number two choice. If that guy's covered he can check down to number three. He's got a prioritized list of who he's going to look to throw to every time they have a passing play.

We invest a lot of time and money attracting all kinds of motivated sellers. When a seller calls us the first check-down we use is Acquisition. We want to buy it. Depending on how motivated they are, we seek to purchase the property because that's usually the highest return on investment. Now, if the seller is not motivated to give us a good enough price or to accept some creative terms, we might have to check down to tying the property up with a contract to get a price or terms we know that we could flip to another investor.

I might only be willing to buy an asset at a certain price, but I might know somebody who will pay more than me. That's often the case because we're very conservative and very aggressive in how we buy property. If I can't get a good enough deal, I'm going to negotiate to tie it up to flip it to somebody else.

The next check-down system: If I can't get an acceptable price or terms to flip that contract, and they just want full retail, I will tell the seller I'll just list his property and find him another buyer.

If you don't have a broker's license, you can structure your check down #3 in such a way where you get a marketing fee or perhaps even a flex option fee for having the rights.

If you have a motivated seller call you, you should be making money one way or another on every single deal.

Not long ago, I interviewed a guy who came into my office. He was applying for an acquisition manager position. He had worked for a company called Prudential and was an acquisition manager for a pension fund.

The number one job of a pension fund is to not lose any money because they are managing a lot of people's guaranteed retirement funds. In fact, the number one job of any investment company is not to not lose any money. Don't lose money, right? Making a profit is great, but if you're losing money, then you will not be in business very long.

I asked the acquisition manager from the Prudential Pension Fund about the real estate portfolio they had, and he said, "The reason pension funds buy apartment buildings is because they're safe, secure, stable, and a hedge against inflation." He said, "It is so hard to lose money on an apartment building. Even if you pay a reasonable price, it's very hard to lose money on an apartment building."

I took this as affirmation that we must be doing something right.

APARTMENT INVESTING

When the market crashed in 2008, I was a condo developer, and I like to say that I lived to tell about it.

The reality is, many developers and house flippers went out of business overnight when the market crashed in

2008. Most people didn't necessarily have a bad deal, but when financing dried up, and the financial markets began to free fall, a lot of people, especially in real estate, got hurt.

I looked around and saw all my compatriots who owned apartment buildings doing very well. As more and more people lost their homes to foreclosure the demand for rental housing began to climb; and so did the value of apartment buildings.

It was then that I knew I would be an apartment owner and grow a massive portfolio.

I like apartment buildings because:

Apartments are one of the safest, most secure, and stable asset classes, even among equities and bonds and other Wall-Street-type investments.

They are the last asset class in real estate to decline when the market crashes; they are the first asset class to rebound when the market corrects. This happens every time, and the logic behind this is pretty simple. Humans need housing, and when the market crashes and people are losing their houses to foreclosure, apartments are a good choice for those looking for a more affordable option. When we compare apartment buildings as an asset class against commercial property, we see that when the economy gets slow, businesses in retail, office and industrial spaces, begin to downsize or close. And when people downsize, they rent apartments.

Another thing I love about owning apartment buildings is that they are a hedge against inflation. When the price of everything goes up (milk, gasoline, tuition, etc.) so goes rents.

Because rents rise with inflation, an inflationary market is not only good for your property values, but it will also increase your revenue.

Apartment investing is one of the best investment products on the planet, even compared to stocks, bonds, mutual funds, gold, whatever. Apartments are fantastic.

A few times a year, I teach a course on Multifamily Mastery. In Multifamily Mastery, you'll learn everything you need to know about buying apartment buildings; selecting a Target Market, how to value a property, how to negotiate the best deal (and yes! You can use all the techniques found in my Creative Real Estate Financing program.) I even show you how to flip, or wholesale, apartment deals.

I give you all the documents, spreadsheets, cheat sheets, and underwriting tools you need to get started and I even throw in incredible marketing tools I use to attract motivated apartment owners.

This is a complete course that also teaches you how to get bank financing (even if you have no money or credit) and how to raise private equity for your down payment.

I always say, "Real estate is a Team Sport" and that is especially true when you graduate from doing little deals into the big leagues of buying (or flipping) apartment buildings.

You can learn more about Multifamily Mastery at DealMakerSociety.com

Conclusion

The Foundation

Throughout this book, we've discussed different tactics and techniques for you to get more organized, be a better communicator, have more influence, and to get more of what you want.

We discovered the Five Pillars to BEING, DOING, and HAVING everything you want in life...

But what is the foundation that these Five Pillars stand on?

Integrity

Integrity is the unwavering commitment to doing the right thing over the convenient thing; it's doing what you said you would do, even after it's no longer in your best interest; its being true especially when it's difficult.

The first place we must practice integrity is with ourselves.

How many times have we promised to start that new diet or exercise program "tomorrow?"

Or what about drinking less? Going to bed earlier? Working harder? Donating or tithing to that certain cause that we claim means so much to us?

Integrity starts with yourself; your inner game.

What goes on inside yourself manifests itself around you; and permeates into your circle of influence.

If you cannot keep promises to yourself, why would your children, wife, or significant other believe you will keep ALL promises to them? And if the people that care about you the most question your integrity, what do you think your competitors or clients will think?

Trust is the new currency and integrity is like your virginity; you can only lose it once.

When you follow the steps in this book, you will be a more powerful person and with that comes great responsibility so I leave you with a difficult challenge: Make promises to yourself now. And practice keeping those promises to yourself daily. People around you will notice; and they will begin to trust you like they trust the sun to rise in the east every morning.

Make Integrity the rock upon which you build your castle.

Master the Five Pillars:

- ✓ BE a great marketer
- ✓ BE a great salesman
- ✓ BE a great negotiator
- ✓ BE a great manager
- ✓ BE financially intelligent

BEING that person is BEING a DEALMAKER.

Then you can DO and HAVE everything you want in life.

About Matt Skinner

Best known as the leader of the controversial, secret real estate club, "DealMaker Society," Matt Skinner is a DealMaking expert, real estate magnate, and the host of the live TV show, Real Talk LIVE. He's founded multiple successful companies, although most famously Empire West Investments and DealMaker Enterprises. Over the years, he's shared his penchant for real estate and business as a university lecturer (most recently Harvard University) and leader of multiple real estate investment groups throughout Southern California. Although he began, with only a shovel in his hand (literally), he's amassed hundreds of millions in real estate assets and has created a vivid imprint on the landscape of real estate investment. He is the epitome of the "American Dream."

After the recession, Matt proceeded to seek out like-minded real estate entrepreneurs for joint ventures and has successfully engineered a network of "DealMakers" across the country. Since then, he's prided himself on mentoring aspiring real estate entrepreneurs to realize their own unprecedented successes. Those able to get a seat at the table in his secret society know he's never been one to shy away from a negotiation, or bold make decisions, that have since led to extensive company expansion into development here in the United States, before going international.

To learn more about joining Matt Skinner's Secret Real Estate Society go to:

DealMakerSociety.com

To find out if investing alongside Matt Skinner financially would be a good fit for you, go to:

MattSkinnerInvestments.com

You can also find Matt Skinner at:

Facebook.com/MattSkinnerInvestments

LinkedIn.com/in/MattSkinner12

Instagram.com/MattSkinner.Dealmaker

http://bit.ly/MattSkinnerYouTube

(310)365-9450

Made in the USA
San Bernardino, CA
13 October 2017